AF254818

Money
Rewritten

Money
Rewritten

Carrie KC West

TRCPRODUCTIONS

For anyone who is tired of money running the show.

Table of Contents

Forward

Over the course of my 33-year professional career, I have had the opportunity to work closely with a diverse range of people. As a private wealth advisor, I carry a profound responsibility to help individuals and families secure their financial futures. While markets, strategies, and performance matter, the real challenge has always been navigating the unique perspectives, experiences, and beliefs each client brings into the relationship.

My effectiveness as an advisor is directly tied to my ability to understand what I call a person's "money story." Every investor carries a story shaped by a lifetime of experiences related to spending, saving, investing, and giving. Culture, race, generation, social class, gender, religion, and pivotal money events all play a role in shaping how someone thinks and feels about money, whether they are consciously aware of it or not. The ability to grasp this complexity, and to meet people where they truly are, has proven to be one of the most important differentiators in my work.

I have had the privilege of knowing and collaborating with Carrie since 2004. Over the years, we have worked together on projects rooted in philanthropy, finance, and mentorship, and I have witnessed firsthand the depth and originality of her approach to serving others. Carrie has an uncommon ability to help people see what has been shaping their decisions beneath the surface, without judgment or oversimplification. This book reflects that same commitment. It is a genuine gift for those who are truly ready to engage with their financial health and well-being in a meaningful way.

In my work advising private business owners, company founders, serial entrepreneurs, entertainment professionals, and athletes, I have remained focused on both the emotional and financial dimensions of wealth throughout every stage of a client's life. Generating strong, risk-adjusted performance is an essential part of the job, but performance alone is rarely what determines long-term success. Client advocacy is often the true difference maker, and advocacy only happens when an advisor understands how a client thinks about money and how those beliefs influence decisions across every area of life.

The most productive and lasting progress occurs when advisors and clients engage in deep, honest conversations about personal history, values, fears, and aspirations around money. These conversations are not always easy, but they are essential. *Money Rewritten* serves as a practical and accessible guide for having those conversations not only with an advisor, but also with family members and trusted individuals within one's inner circle. It provides language, structure, and clarity for discussions that many people sense are important yet struggle to initiate.

One of the questions I am asked most frequently is, "What makes someone a successful investor, and why do some people achieve financial independence while others never seem to get there?" My answer often surprises people. While intelligence, income, and access to opportunity matter, the most influential factor is a person's relationship with money itself. Left unexamined, many individuals fall into the recurring pull of fear and greed. This cycle can repeat for years, even decades, leading to decisions that undermine long-term goals and create unnecessary stress and regret.

The good news is that a relationship with money is not set in stone. It can evolve. Awareness creates choice, and choice creates the possibility for better outcomes. This is where *Money Rewritten* stands apart. The book brings clarity to the invisible forces that quietly drive financial behavior and offers a way forward that feels grounded, realistic, and attainable. It does not rely on hype or promises of quick fixes. Instead, it invites readers to understand themselves more deeply so they can make decisions that are aligned with who they are and where they want to go.

Over the years, I have read countless books that promise financial success and personal change. Many are well intentioned, but most fall short because they lack a practical framework for creating lasting change. They sound good but leave readers without a clear path forward. Carrie offers something different. She presents a thoughtful, actionable approach that honors both the emotional and practical realities of money. More importantly, she reminds readers that meaningful change is not only possible, but worth the effort.

Money Rewritten is not about perfection. It is about progress, awareness, and building a healthier relationship with money over time. For those who are willing to engage honestly and do the work, this book can mark the beginning of a more confident, intentional, and independent financial life.

Brian Werdesheim
Managing Director/Investments
Stifel | The Summa Group

Introduction

Here's the truth most people don't want to admit: your relationship with money runs your life far more than money itself ever will.

It shapes how you work, how you love, how you sleep at night, how you feel when you open your banking app, and who you believe you're allowed to be in the world. Most of us walk around thinking we're stressed about the numbers, but the numbers are rarely the real problem. It's the story underneath. It's the emotions we never question. It's the quiet beliefs we picked up long before we earned our first paycheck. It's the reason why we believe we are in the situation we're in.

When I decided to write a book about money, I wasn't interested in how to manage or budget. I wanted to understand why I had spent decades worrying about money, chasing it, grabbing it, losing it, and never feeling like I had enough — even during the times when everything on paper said I did. I lived in a constant tape loop of anxiety, ambition, and desperation. And I thought that was just how life worked.

Then something unexpected happened. I got tired. I was over the constant mind games running around in my head. So I stopped and accepted that maybe this was my life. I decided to focus on things that made me happy — our new puppy, community work, the creative projects I put in my 'someday when' bucket. I was writing my first book, *Life Rewritten,* and as I dug into the stories I was handed about life, money started behaving differently. It began to show up in ways I couldn't ignore. I'd been putting money aside for a tax bill, and instead I received a refund of over ten thousand dollars. I sold my condo at the highest price per square foot in the entire association — after everyone told me it was the worst possible time to sell. My bills went down. My savings went up. And for the first time in my adult life, money felt… calmer.

It became clear that the more mental energy I put into chasing money, the harder it ran from me. The moment I shifted my focus, my relationship with money shifted too.

If you're like most people, money brings up a whole range of emotions — fear, anxiety, excitement, shame, guilt, confusion. Whether you're comfortable or barely keeping things together, money has a way of demanding your attention. Our culture only makes it worse. If you have money, people assume you're lucky or blessed. If you don't, you are judged about your discipline, your intelligence, or your worth. These labels stick. They become part of your story, even when they're untrue and long past their relevance.

But here's the part nobody teaches you: money has no story. It has no meaning. No motive. No agency. Money isn't the villain or the hero. It just exists. What creates all the noise — the fear, the pressure, the shame — is our relationship with it. That's where the trouble begins. And that's where the rewrite starts.

Money is simply a form of exchange, a practical way to trade value without dragging a cart of goats around every time you need groceries. That's all it is. Yet somehow we've layered meaning onto money that it was never designed to carry. We treat it as proof of success or evidence of failure, a sign of virtue or a mark of shame. The old phrase "money is the root of all evil" gets repeated like gospel, even though the original text says, "the love of money is the root of all evil." That tiny difference says everything. Money isn't the problem. Our obsession with it is. The preoccupation, the chasing, the fear — that's where we get tangled.

And that distinction, the one between money as a tool and money as a reflection, is the purpose of this book. I've come to believe that most of what we inherit about money is outdated, inaccurate, or just plain wrong. But we absorb it anyway because these beliefs show up early — long before any of us are conscious enough to question them. As children, we pick up messages about wealth and lack, about who deserves what, about whether wanting more is ambition or greed. These stories don't just shape how we behave with money; they shape how we see ourselves. Sometimes they push us to achieve more. Other times they give us limits we don't even realize are holding us back.

Once you begin questioning these old ideas, something shifts. Money loses its mystery. It becomes less of a judgement and more of a resource — one that can support your life or complicate it depending on how you relate to it. Yes, money pays for your life. It keeps the lights on, feeds your family, and opens doors. But it doesn't define you. It doesn't decide your worth. And it doesn't need to be the thing you dread, chase, or obsess over.

My goal in *Money Rewritten* is to help you take a closer look at the stories you've been carrying — where they came from, how they're running the show, and which ones are ready to be thrown out. Whether you're buried in debt, earning well but still feeling broke, trying to build savings, or just exhausted from thinking about money all the time, you can rewrite the narrative. You can create a new way of relating to money that actually supports you.

If *Life Rewritten* was an invitation to question the stories you inherited about life itself, *Money Rewritten* brings that same experience to your financial world. Your attitudes about money shape everything — your confidence, your security, your choices, your future. When you shift that relationship, you shift your entire experience of your life.

By the end of this book, my goal for you is this: you will feel less tied up with angst around money and see it more for what it truly is – a tool, a resource that's here for you to use with confidence and clarity. You'll see where you've been holding yourself back and where you can open to something new. Money can flow into your life more easily when you stop letting old stories block the way. You can be as abundant as you choose. You can have as much of the life you want. You just have to change the reasons why not.

That's the work you'll do here.

My Approach

It starts with awareness. Before you can change anything about your relationship with money, you have to understand what you're actually dealing with — not just the numbers, but the stories, emotions, and beliefs underneath them. That's why this book begins by looking at what money really is and how it became such a powerful force. Once that foundation is in place, I'll invite you to uncover your own money origin story. This is the one you perceived and absorbed by observing the world around you before you had words and choices. You learned more about money in your earliest years than you ever learned from a paycheck or a bank statement.

Those early messages still control your reactions today. When you can finally see those behaviors, you can start dismantling them, piece by piece. You'll look at the role money plays in your life, the language you use, and the ways you allow (or block) money from coming in. And from there, you'll see where your story can shift.

Some of this work might stir things up. That's normal. In my master classes, people often arrive holding tight to money beliefs they never chose or knew they had. They leave with a clarity and ease they didn't think was possible. You can have that same experience here, in your own way, at your own pace.

Structure of the Book

Just like in *Life Rewritten* each chapter begins with a story from my life that showed how I thought about money long before I knew why. The stories are true, though I've changed names to respect people's privacy. There are times I combined some of the narratives to make for ease of storytelling, but all events are as I experienced them. After each story, I walk you through the idea behind it: what it meant for me, and what it might show you.

Then, at the end of every chapter, you'll find a "What's Your Story" section. This is your space to reflect, write, sketch, record — whatever helps you explore your own money narrative. These steps are meant to help you see your patterns, question the messages you've carried, and start rewriting the parts of your story that no longer fit.

A Final Thought Before We Begin

Money is often treated like a report card or judgement. But that's not what it is. This book isn't about fixing you, forcing discipline, or teaching you to squeeze yourself into someone else's idea of success. It's about seeing the truth of your relationship with money — where it came from, how it works, and how you can create something healthier and more aligned with who you are now.

You don't have to keep living the story you inherited. You get to rewrite it.

Beginning now.

For additional help, PDF downloads, resources and information on how to go further on your journey, visit my website carriekcwest.com where you'll find courses, ideas and support. For your convenience, you can use the QR Code below:

Chapter 1
What is Money?

*"Money makes the world go round." —**Cabaret***

September 1976

Economics 101 was one of those basic requirements everyone had to take to get a degree. I never understood if it was just meant to torture students or if educators honestly believed a well-rounded education that prepared us for life had to include economics. Even if it was the latter, as I sat in that large auditorium packed with bored, uninterested students, I saw no point in knowing how our financial systems operated.

The professor at the front of the room wrote unintelligible concepts on the board that made my head hurt. Like macro vs micro-economics, law of supply and demand, zero sum game… I took notes only because these things would be on some future test, but like many of the others around me, I fought to stay awake.

My mind wandered. Economics was about money, right? I mean we're in the United Stated where capitalism supposedly ran the show and everyone had a chance to make as much money as they wanted, right? So why were there so many poor people? Why were so many college students like me taking out loans just to get an education my parents couldn't afford?

I honestly can't remember a time when my parents could afford anything. I didn't have birthday parties or vacations so why would they help me with school? It was always on me to pay my own way. So how was I supposed to get more? I wanted more. I wanted a lot more. And I'd been told the only way to get ahead was to get a good education, so there I was. But did this boring teacher have any clue how to turn market efficiency into a bigger paycheck? Did anyone really know how money worked? People who had it seemed to get more of it, while the rest of us had to make do. Was that the truth about capitalism, or was there some other system that could actually give me a shot?

If I could answer that question, I'd sell it and make a million bucks. But who was I kidding? My head was spinning just trying to follow this guy talk about market fluctuations. None of it made sense to me. Nothing about money made sense to me.

The Allure of Money

The notion of money is one that permeates everyone's thoughts. For many of us, we learn about money the same way we learn language: by observation. I remember my parents talking about money problems late into the night and discovered that many people I know had the same memories. I remember the first time my mom gave me a quarter to get penny candy at the drugstore. I was in seventh heaven. For the first time I had the power to buy something I wanted, something for me. I liked feeling that power, that control over my life, my choices.

I remember the time when I was ten years old and Dad in a rare moment of vulnerability apologized to me for not being able to afford many of the normal things in life like new clothes and toys or how he wouldn't be able to afford a car for me or my younger sister, Tessa, when the time came. I remember him saying that he just wasn't motivated enough to make any more money no matter what that meant for his family. I remember the shame I felt when I wore hand-me-down clothes that never seemed to fit very well or that Mom bought my shoes on sale whether they fit me or not.

But what is money? Before you can understand your money stories and the effect they have on your life, you need to know what money is. In my experience, money was what you needed to live. Over time, though, economics and finance grew into entire industries that turned money into something far bigger than an exchange of value. Money became a force, shaping lives and decisions in ways we couldn't imagine. Today, we don't just use money — we manage it, strategize around it, and measure ourselves by it. We compare our worth to others based on how much we have and what we do with it. For many, money isn't a supporting character; it's the A-list star, on our minds daily — if not constantly.

In and of itself, money is a concept. It's intangible in that it has no physical form. Currency, cash – in the form of bills and coins – and credit cards are tangible representations of money and often used to reference the amount of money someone has at their disposal. The concept of money is used to explain a system that allows for the exchange of value given for value received. It can be a purchase or a salary for services performed. The need to exchange value for value started out thousands of years ago as a bartering system.

Before we had a physical means to represent the value exchange, people would barter goods and services. For example, farmers could exchange crops for goods and services needed. Say a farmer needed a new tool for the farm, if they couldn't build it, they'd need to trade for it, often using cows or pigs to get a new scythe. But bartering is limited in that people would need to find someone that wanted the goods they had and could provide the service that was sought. The solution came when societies developed other ways to represent value in exchanges. Using metal pieces of fixed weight and value began thousands of years ago in an area of Turkey that was known as Lydia. Having a coin that carried an agreed upon value meant that the country could accumulate wealth, making the area one of the richest empires of its time.

Later, the Yuan Dynasty of China started using an early form of paper money that eventually caught on around the world. The earliest paper currency was handled by the banks and private organizations until the governments of countries took control of the process.

There was a time when the currency that was used carried the value backed by what was known as "the gold standard." Each bank note represented a specific amount of gold held by the government. In the United States, Fort Knox still holds over half of the of the federal government's gold reserve. Even so, over time "money" took on a life of its own so much so that the dollar bills in your wallet aren't a representation of gold at Fort Knox. Markets shifted. Economies grew. Value was tied not just to currencies but to stocks, bonds, and commodities. Most of the money we use today exists digitally in bank accounts, not as physical cash. It's backed not by a physical commodity but by the full faith and credit of the government that issues it.

And this is where many people forget something important: "money" doesn't run around freely on its own. It exists inside an economy that governments are constantly managing. Interest rates rise, inflation shifts, the flow of money expands or con-tracts — and much of what we experience as "money anxiety" is really our reaction to those shifts, not a personal failing.

As our need for faster and easier ways to exchange value for value grew, we became increasingly dependent on the *concept* of money. We agreed collectively on the value of the dollar, even though nothing 'real' backs it anymore.

And as that agreement grew, people, businesses, and nations began hoarding money in all its forms — sometimes for pro-gress, sometimes for power. Money came to represent safety. Money became a marker of status, shaping how we see ourselves and how others see us. Money came to represent love and fair-ness. When we feel wronged, we seek compensation through the courts, even when the losses are intangible. When we succeed, we expect bonuses and payouts.

At certain points in life, money takes center stage. Marriage can bring prenuptial agreements or decisions about whether to blend finances. Parenthood forces us to consider long-term financial stability. Divorce often turns into battles over shared assets. Health crises or unexpected tragedies can drive even the most stable household toward financial ruin.

We absorbed ideas about money the same way we learned language — through family, culture, and community. What we saw, what we heard, what we lived. Those stories became part of us, so deeply embedded that changing our response to money — to having it, holding it, or going after it — can feel impossible.

But it isn't. That's why *Money Rewritten* begins with this chapter. Understanding how money -- a piece of paper, a metal coin, a piece of plastic or a digital notch in a data file – has become such a force… and then how you can change your relationship with it.

The Plot Thickens

Every great story starts with understanding the world we're playing in and so this brief history of money was important. We need to know how we got here. We also need to know that money is an exchange of value for value. We've given currencies value, we've made credit a valuable asset so much so that credit card companies and banks are among the wealthiest in the world. They're essentially using money to accumulate more money in a relentless and fascinating cycle.

This is where things get interesting. Once money stopped being just a tool and instead became a system in itself, it shaped not only economies but our imaginations, our fears and our choices. That's where we begin to see how deeply money has infiltrated our stories.

Cultures are measured by it – think of the contrasts between wealthy nations and so called developing "third world" countries. Wars have been fought over the control of gold, oil (sometimes referred to as 'liquid gold'), trade routes and other symbols of financial power. We perceive people with large sums of money as "privileged" while those with less economic standing as "marginalized." Some societies view money as immoral while others see it as a form of divine favor.

Money even has a language all its own: afford, expensive, debt and more. Knowing the language you use is critical to understanding your relationship with money. We take pride in how much money we have how we manage it and how well we make it work for us. Is it any wonder that our money stories need to be examined and rewritten?

Plot Points

To recap:

- Money is an imaginary construct, an energetic pattern that is given a great deal of power over what you feel and think about your life.

- Money is an exchange of value for value but somewhere along the line it became a measurement of self-worth.

- Your personal value is not tied to the amount of money you have in the bank.

What's Your Story

Each chapter ends with a section called: What's Your Story. This is your chance to consider and apply the ideas to your own life. I recommend capturing your thoughts in whatever way works for you: journals, sketching, collages, etc. I work with someone that records on her phone, giving voice to her thoughts. Do what works for you, after all, this section is for you.

Thinking about money and its history think about these steps:

Step 1: What's your view of money in your own life and in the world? Are there other ideas you would add to what you've read so far?

Step 2: What role has money had in your life?

Step 3: What shifts do you imagine are possible in your relationship with money? Where would you start?

This is the starting point on your journey of rewriting your money story. Don't force it or try to edit it. Let your story reveal itself.

Chapter 2
Money Origin Stories

"Show me the money!"
—**Rod Tidwell,** *Jerry Maguire*

October 1959

Sleep escaped me. I had no idea what time it was. Mom always wanted us to be in bed by nine o'clock. I think it was because she wanted the peace and quiet without any of us around. Tessa was just over a year old and was in her crib in the room she shared with our brother Mark. Sally and I shared a room, but I never trusted Sally and would try to stay awake until she fell asleep. She already tried to get Mark to put a pillow over my head and suffocate me. When Mom saw what was going on, she yelled and Mark said that Sally gave him a quarter to do it.

While I waited for sleep, I could hear voices from the living room. It wasn't a big house and noise carried easily. Mom and

Dad were having a familiar talk about the bills and money, or rather the fact that money was 'tight.' Even at almost three years old my concepts of money were forming and I wondered how it could be tight. Mom wasn't happy that Dad wouldn't work overtime to get more money to cover the bills. Dad wasn't interested and said that they'd have to cut back.

Mom's voice raised as she said, "Cut back?! Where else can I cut back? We need money for food and gas just rose to twenty-three cents a gallon. Sally and Mark have grown out of all their clothes and I need some new slacks. We pay $200 a month for the house and then the utilities are another $25… I can't make what you bring home stretch any further."

Dad was unmoved. "You'll figure something out. Maybe you don't go to Bingo three times a week."

That did it. "You'd deny me the one thing I love in this shitty life. We don't do anything or go anywhere. I'm stuck here all day with these four brats while you're out all day and then you come home and go to the club! If you're not careful, I'll go get a job on my own and leave you to take care of the house."

It was quiet for a moment. "I can't keep having this conversation. You tricked me into having more kids so you have to live with it. You made your bed now sleep in it. I'm going to bed."

I listened as Dad walked into his room, Moments later a loud snore filled the air. I rolled over on my side and put my thumb in my mouth.

The Value of Origin Stories

You can easily trace nearly every money issue back to your origin stories. Origin stories are the foundation of who you are. From the moment you are born, it's as if you stepped onto a stage where the play has been running for decades. Your arrival into the middle of the second act means the plot and the themes are already well established; the other characters already well-versed in the action underway. Your role is at first undefined, but you aren't given the luxury of time to learn the play and come up with your place in the story. Instead, you are expected to catch up quickly, to absorb the storylines, learn the rules and make sense of the meanings and motivations. In those early years you soak up everything – not just the words and actions, but all the emotions whirling around you. These become the scripts that reflect the choices, decisions and beliefs you hold about life – including your thoughts and attitudes around money.

Belonging

One of the strongest forces in your life is the craving for a sense of belonging. As children, this need drives the urgency that allows you to accept what you observe and are told without question. Belonging is one of the most basic human needs. It's vital to feel connected to others around you; your family is the first step in establishing that bond. When you take the next step in socialization – through school, friendships and social inter-actions, the scripts you developed become even more essential. These scripts act as a guide informing us on how we behave and respond in daily life.

Part of belonging also means learning who's in and who's out. These messages aren't meant to be harsh. They are often handed down subconsciously or unconsciously as part of the survival code of fitting in. You may have been told either through language or observation, that people who look different, live differently or hold different values can't be trusted or worse, are to be feared. Not everyone looks like you or speaks the same language or believes as you do. But instead of looking for commonality, you're told to be wary.

It's the same with our money. Just as you are taught who belongs and who doesn't, you also inherit unspoken rules about money. You tend to gravitate towards others that hold similar attitudes, reinforcing what you've absorbed.

Here's a scenario from one of my clients.

JD's Story

JD had a solid job and earned a mid-range salary. She loved her work and was seemingly happy with her life. Her life changed when she met a man who had a great deal of money. He traveled the world and had a lifestyle far beyond hers. They began dating and over time, JD wondered about a future together.

When she told her parents, though, they dismissed her dream. They believed the gap in social status and income was impossible to overcome. No matter how much JD argued, her parents were not convinced. "It won't work," they told her – not because of who he was – they, in fact, thought he was a kind and generous person. But they argued, "Status and money rule the day."

JD decided to continue the relationship until one day, he ended it. She was devastated. Three months later she discovered that he was engaged to a young socialite who was a family friend. JD's immediate thought was, *"My parents were right."*

The Underlying Narrative

When JD came to me she was heartbroken. We worked on her origin story with a focus on her family's relationship with money. She realized that deep down she had doubted herself all along. She didn't feel equal to him, deferred to him and lacked confidence. She had set the stage for the relationship to fail from the very beginning.

Over time, JD saw that her parents weren't being cruel. They were repeating the money messages they themselves had inherited. Their warnings were ingrained in a belief system designed to protect her from disappointment, but in doing so, they substantiated her limitations. They handed her a worn and tattered script about social inequality and money, one that was written to keep her small, and she believed it.

While noble in its intention, JD's parents instilled in her limitations around money,

Effects on Adulthood

JD started dissecting her origin story. She saw how her parents' messages weren't new; they had been passed down for generations. Repeated often enough, those inherited beliefs became entrenched in her psyche, guiding her choices and undermining her confidence.

Through forgiveness, compassion, and new awareness, JD began to release the shame and regret she carried. She came to see the relationship not as a failure, but as a learning experience, an opportunity to make a new decisions. It revealed how her money scripts had shaped her choices, and it gave her the power to change them.

The result was life-changing. JD not only healed her heartbreak but also expanded her vision of what was possible. She pursued a higher-paying job, was hired by a top company, and received a 30% salary increase plus a signing bonus. More importantly, she stepped into her own sense of worth — no longer defined by someone else's script.

Just as JD's story shows you, your money origin stories are alive in you today. They show up in relationships, career and in how you think about your worth. The good news is that by uncovering them, you can decide which stories to keep and which ones to rewrite.

The Plot Thickens
My Family's Money Origin Story

Mom and Dad were first generation American's. Dad's family was from Italy. They emigrated to America and landed in Pittsburgh Pennsylvania. I never knew why they came to Pittsburgh except that it was well-known for its thriving Italian neighborhood. Dad's father was a trained barber. He set up shop and had a prosperous business in the city. Dad was born in 1920 joining his older sister who arrived three years earlier.

Mom's family was from Serbia. They settled in a small town in Western Pennsylvania called Josephine. They acquired land and went to work farming. They raised crops and had a few cows, chickens and pigs. Mom was born in 1921, one of thirteen children. The children took care of the animals and worked wherever needed.

Both families were impacted by the Great Depression though in different ways. Dad's family had to find new ways to make money when the barber shop lost clients and had to close. Grandpa Frank took to running numbers for local gambling games popular in Italian American communities.

Mom's family faced hardships even before 1929. Farming was difficult and supporting a family and looking for ways to survive was an essential and ongoing task. As the family grew and the children left to their own lives, Grandad Michael went to work in the coal mines of Western Pennsylvania with two of his sons.

Neither of my parents had more than an eighth-grade education. They needed to work as soon as they could to bring money in for the family. Dad got his taste for gambling watching the men his dad worked for and observing the amount of money that could be made effortlessly. Dad was also a genius with numbers. He could see a list of numbers and tally them in head without paper and pencil. It served him well for his poker games.

Mom resented farm life. She had big dreams of wealth and luxury. When she was 18, she went to New York City with two of her sister's seeking housework, preferably with a wealthy family. Mom and her sisters were beautiful: tall, fair-haired with high cheekbones. Mom was sure she'd land herself a rich man who'd buy her beautiful clothes and jewelry. She dreamt of a glamorous life. It didn't work out that way. When one of her sisters married a man from Brooklyn the other decided to move to Pittsburgh and took my mom with her. Mom found a job at a local A&P Grocery and rose to become the manager of the candy department.

Dad in the meantime, got a job driving a truck for A&P. He hated it, but his dad told him he had to get a job and give up any dreams of gambling. What Grandpa Frank didn't know was that every weekend Dad was playing cards. He was great at poker, but his real game was pinochle. His ability to memorize cards aligned perfectly with his math skills. Plus gambling made him feel clever and important.

Mom and Dad met at A&P and eventually married. Dad kept the job he hated so that he had benefits for his family but played poker most nights at the local club. He turned the basement of our house into a game room. He paneled the walls, added a bar and built a poker table. Once a month strangers came through our garage into the updated room. The following morning, the room smelled of cigars and whiskey. When I was ten years old, Dad quit his job at A&P and increased the frequency of the poker games. On these nights, Dad didn't play; he instead took a cut of every pot. The next day he'd leave Mom a stack of bills on the kitchen table while he slept in.

Money was always tight. I remember Mom kept a small yellow notepad of the bills she paid each month. She'd keep a list of the amount that went to the mortgage, utilities, groceries and other expenses. We never went on vacation just the occasional day trips to Mom's family who lived nearby. One year, Dad drove us to New York to see my Aunt Jo and her family. Dad drove straight through on the Pennsylvania Turnpike and was ready to leave almost as soon as we arrived.

We didn't get many new things. Our clothes were usually hand-me-downs from older cousins. Our home furnishings came from Mom's tireless effort to collect the green stamps she received from grocery and gas purchases. After she accumulated enough books, we'd go to the redemption center to purchase something for the house. Tessa and I loved to go with her. We looked at all the amazing things on the shelves and wondered what Mom would bring home.

But something always struck me when we left the redemption center. Mom wasn't excited about her purchases. She seemed sad and never talked much on the way home.

After Dad quit his job at A&P, money was even tighter. There was a time when all our dinners consisted of iceberg lettuce and pasta. After months of eating like this we were invited to a barbecue at my Aunt Marte's. I ate three hamburgers savoring each bite. Not long after that, Mom got a job in the deli department at a local grocers. She brought home $100 a week and all the luncheon meats we wanted.

When I was older and saw the things the other girls in school had, I asked Mom why I didn't have so many nice things like other people had. Mom became angry. She looked directly at me and said, "You have a roof over your head and food on the table. What else do you need?"

My Origin Story

Once I really understood my family's story, a lot of my own behavior made sense. My parents came from two very different worlds, but the money patterns they brought into adulthood had the same bottom line: survival.

Dad grew up watching money come and go in waves. His father had a good barbershop until the Depression wiped it out, and suddenly the family had to get creative to keep food on the table. For my dad, the "creative" part turned into gambling. He was brilliant with numbers and could track cards better than anyone, so winning felt natural to him. It also made him feel important. That mattered to him.

Mom came from a huge Serbian farm family where everyone worked and still struggled. She dreamed of something bigger and envied those born into wealth. She wanted a life where you didn't spend every day worrying. But in reality she worked at grocery store, saving green stamps to furnish the house and stretching every dollar as far as it could go.

That's the environment I grew up in: a dad who chased money through cards and chance, and a mom who tried to make the most of every penny she earned. In our family we were shown that you were either lucky with money or born lucky. We weren't either, and it took a toll.

And even though we didn't talk about money directly, the messages were loud.

Work hard. Don't expect too much. Be grateful for what you have. Wanting more is a fool's errand. Having more makes you a target.

When I was ten-years old, Dad apologized to me for not doing more. "I'm just not interested in providing anything beyond the food you eat and the home where you live." Between his words and Mom's I learned that seeking abundance was just not in my future. The message was clear. I needed to accept the life I was born into.

So when I became an adult, I carried all of that with me. I didn't know how to think about money in a healthy way. I didn't know how to plan for the future because no one in my life had ever had the luxury of thinking ahead. They were too busy figuring out the week.

By the time I hit my thirties, I finally bought a car I'd always dreamed of. A Porsche. And instead of celebrating, I hid it. I didn't want my family to know. I could already hear the comments, the judgment, the guilt. "If you have that kind of money, why aren't you helping us?" The truth was I didn't have any money. I had a loan and a great car. I had no savings. No retirement plan. No clue about financial security. I only knew how to repeat what I had learned: get a job you don't like, put up with it, save just enough to quit when you can't take it anymore, and then hope some kind of miracle opportunity or scheme shows up.

Looking back, I can see exactly where that came from. I was living the story I inherited. Dad's gamble for the big win. Mom's belief that wanting more was dangerous. The constant focus on "just enough" and nothing beyond it.

That story shaped every financial decision I made without me even realizing it. And it kept me small. Confused. Afraid to want more because wanting more felt like breaking some unspoken rule.

And like most inherited stories, it didn't work out the way I hoped. It wasn't sustainable. It wasn't healthy. And it wasn't the life I wanted.

But it was the story I started with and until I knew it and felt it deep in my core, I was destined to live with it.

Plot Points

To recap:

- Your Money Origin Story is a wealth of information that shows you the relationship you have with money in your present day. In my family, abundance was a foreign concept, one that didn't apply to us. It was a direct message from my grandparents who thought that life was about working hard and struggling to make ends meet.

- Discovering your Money Origin Story is the first step in changing your relationship with money.

- Working with your Money Origin Story impacts every aspect of your life due to money's effect on how you feel, think and imagine who you are. Changing the story changes the other aspects of your life as well.

What's Your Story

Follow each of the steps below to uncover and begin working with your Money Origin Story.

Step 1: What is the first thing you remember about money? It could be a phrase you heard or a memory like the one I shared about hearing my parents talking about money at night. Describe what you remember in as much detail as possible.

Step 2: Did you receive an allowance? If so, how old were you and what was the amount? Was your allowance tied to doing chores or was it given freely?

Step 3: Did you work any small jobs growing up to make money? Did you babysit? Mow lawns? Have a paper route? What was it like to earn money in that way? I remember when I made two dollars babysitting when I was eleven years old. I felt like I had all the money in the world and couldn't wait to spend it on something I wanted – not something Mom thought I should have. How did having money feel to you? Compare it to how it felt to have an allowance.

Step 4: List any idea around money that parents, extended family or teachers stated repeatedly. It might include one of these phrases:

- Money doesn't grow on trees!
- We can't afford that?
- Who do you think you are, the Rockefellers? The Kennedy's? The (fill in the name a wealthy family).
- Struggle to make ends meet.
- Other

Step 5: Think about your overall memory of your early years and your relationship with money. Capture your thoughts in a way that works for you. You might journal, draw or record a video. The important thing is to note your story in any way you can.

Our money origin stories are powerful but they aren't perma-nent. In the next chapter we'll look at the role money plays in your life: the antagonist, the foil even the hero.

Chapter 3
Friend or Foe

"Money doesn't change people. It only shows who they really are." —**Bruce Wayne**, *The Dark Knight*

March 1981

$1,500?" I knew the surprise in my voice was laced with shock, disbelief and anger. I wondered, **when was I going to be able to hold onto whatever windfall?** *Just yesterday I found out I was getting $1,200 back from my taxes. Today, I'm sitting in the dentist's chair being told I need a crown that will cost even more. I can hand over the money or ask if they can spread the payments across three credit cards.*

I told myself insurance would help, especially with my dental problems. But I learned quickly that most dentists don't take it, and when they do, it barely helps — it's expensive and usually covers only a third of the cost.

I left my dentist's office frustrated and miserable.

*The errant thoughts came rushing in. **Every time I seemed to get ahead something like this happens.** It never failed. The minute I made a little progress, something unexpected showed up to take it away.*

*This time it was a dental bill. Next time it would be something else. Somehow, money never seemed to want to stay with me. I'd think, **Why does money hate me so much?** I hadn't even received the refund, and it was already gone.*

It wasn't a new story. When I was in third grade, Mom gave me ten dollars to buy my sister Tessa a birthday present — a huge amount to me back then. I found the perfect gift, but when Mom asked for the change, it was gone. Maybe a dollar fifty. I couldn't explain it. She was disappointed, and I was embarrassed.

Maybe that's where it started — the feeling that money and I weren't on the same page. That no matter what I did, it slipped away before I could take a breath.

Money – Leading Character
or Supporting Cast

Just as origin stories define how you view money, the way you cast money in your life gives it a personality. For me, money wasn't a number on a page, it was a character with a starring role.

While I've shared one story of money undermining my plans and ambitions, there were plenty more to choose from. The truth is, I was the one giving money power over my dreams.

If I wanted to join friends on a trip, I'd panic about the cost, fearful of where the next dollar would come from, and convince myself the trip was a bad idea. When I was finally ready to quit a job I hated, the stress of leaving without a safety net held me back. Again and again, I cast money in the role of fiend, the culprit blocking my road to happiness.

Money was always an easy target. When I wanted something but told myself I "couldn't afford it," money became the excuse. Whenever I received a bonus, a raise or financial gift, something else would break or fall apart, wiping it out. I'd wonder, *Why doesn't money like to stay with me?* It felt like the minute I brought any home it went right out the side door.

After a while, the pattern became so familiar that I didn't even wait for the loss. I created it. When I did get a large bonus, I'd find a way to spend it quickly, often on something I didn't want. Somewhere inside, I decided it was better to get rid of the money first rather than wait for life to take it from me.

Money often played the antagonist to my protagonist, making life feel difficult, uncertain, and full of worry. Money became the constant in my mind. I worried about making more, I avoided opening mail for fear it was another bill. I borrowed from Peter to pay Paul, opening credit cards to cover debts. I compared myself to those who seemed to not have a money care in the world, shopping for new clothes and traveling to exciting parts of the world, jealous of their easy lives.

I blamed money and its absence in my life. It became the character that refused to be cast in a long-term, loving role. It was The Villain stealing my peace of mind when all I wanted was The Hero who would rescue me.

The truth is, I gave money all these roles – and many more. I cast it as The Bad Guy when I didn't want to own my role in the story. It was easier to blame money than face the truth, a truth that I learned from my family.

I was afraid to take chances to risk trying something new that had a chance of bringing a richer more fulfilling life. Instead, I shut down. I carried resentment toward my father for not doing more with his life, for not providing a better one for us. For not setting a better example, a stronger path to follow. Until I uncovered that anger – rage really – I followed his same path giving money a starring role in the story of debt and financial stress.

The Plot Thickens

As I said in the introduction, money doesn't have agency – it's energy. It has no will to interfere with or sabotage dreams. It isn't motivated to do anything. It simply *is*. Whatever I say or feel about it doesn't change its nature.

Money doesn't cry if I call it uncaring or heartless. Nor does it celebrate when I add to my IRA or buy a stock that triples in value. Yet money holds a strong role in the lives of many—including myself and the people I work with.

Here's what I've learned: money doesn't make people do strange things. People behave strangely *because* of money. Whether you have more than you know what to do with or you're scrambling to make ends meet, money always finds a way in your story.

That means money—being a concept —gets cast in roles it never auditioned for. You can cast it as the villain, the hero, the temptress, the saboteur. Once you do, the illusion takes hold: you believe it can shape outcomes. But it can't. It truly, honestly cannot. What changes is you. You give it the lines, the power, the influence over how the story unfolds.

So the real question becomes: *what are you avoiding?* What truth are you unwilling to face, that makes it easier to let money take center stage as the distraction, the culprit, the scapegoat?

And let's be clear, this isn't just a problem for people without money. The wealthiest among us can be just as trapped. Having abundance doesn't guarantee happiness or peace of mind. Some people spend extraordinary amounts of time and energy guarding their wealth, suspicious of anyone who gets too close. They may be surrounded by people, yet still wonder: *Do they like me for who I am—or just for my money?*

Take Judy, for example. She was what some would call a "trust fund baby." Her family had amassed significant wealth, and Judy received her own trust fund when she turned eighteen. Later, after her parents passed, she inherited even more. By all accounts, Judy should have been free to enjoy her life. But she wasn't.

When the bill came at dinner with friends, she'd pull out her calculator, tally her exact share, and tip exactly 12.5%—the number her father once told her was fair. She lived in constant fear of catastrophe, convinced some disaster would strip it all away. The fear ran so deep that she never built a career or developed skills of her own. If the money vanished, she'd be destitute. For Judy, money wasn't just a tool—it was a superior being, one that demanded loyalty and obedience.

On the other end of the spectrum was Susan, who approached me after one of my introductory talks. She grew up in a family where money was always scarce. Vacations were luxuries "other people" had. Buying more than a few items of clothing was wasteful, even shameful. One aunt used to scold her for owning more than three skirts: "You can only wear one at a time." For Susan, money was dangerous, even immoral. It was cast as the villain in every story, standing in the way of joy, a constant reminder of her limits.

Different stories. Same pattern. Whether money is abundant or scarce, whether it's cast as hero or villain, the truth remains: the role is given, not earned.

If money has been playing a starring role in your life—whether as villain, protector, or master—you're not alone. We all do it. The question now is: what role have you given money in your story? And how has that casting shaped the choices you've made, the beliefs you've held, and the limits you've lived within?

Plot Points

To recap:

- Money is a construct, plain and simple. It has no agency.

- You give money power over how you feel, how you behave, and how you think about yourself.

- Money becomes the villain only when you make it responsible for your life. It's time to look at why you've given it that responsibility.

What's Your Story

It's time to look at the role you've cast money in within your own life. Consider the following steps:

Step 1: What role has money played in your life? Villain, Hero, Trickster, friend? Or the Love Interest? Note any significant situations and where money appeared and impacted your story.

Step 2: Is there one scene, or several, where money's role is especially clear? Write these down. Do you see a common thread? Is it the same role? Note and discrepancies.

Step 3: Did you assign money that role to avoid facing something else? Be honest about what you might have been unwilling or afraid to see. Note this as well.

In these first three steps, you uncovered where and how money shows up in your life — the roles you've given it and the patterns that keep repeating.

These next two steps are designed to change that. By giving money a form and a voice, you take it out of the abstract and into the familiar. It's no longer a mysterious force you can't control; it becomes something you can see, speak to, and understand.

When you imagine money as a character, you start to recognize the energy and emotion you've attached to it — fear, guilt, frustration, or even longing. Once you can see it, you can work with it. These steps help you build a relationship with money based on awareness rather than anxiety, so you can finally begin to change the story you've been telling about it.

Step 4: Close your eyes and imagine money in the role it has played in your life. Give it a form. Is it a person — male or female? Or something else entirely — a shape, an object, maybe even an animal? Notice how it looks. What is it wearing? Is it holding anything? Let the image fill in naturally. Then talk to it. Ask "Money" about the role it's been playing. Is it enjoying it? What has it learned from the experience? What might it want you to know?

Step 5: Now engage with "Money." What do you say to each other? How does it respond? Let the conversation unfold without trying to control it. Be open to what comes through — the words, the emotions, even the silence. Notice how you feel as you listen. Does the energy shift? Is the relationship changing?

You've now met and spoken with money. Take a moment to reflect on how that experience feels. What surprised you? What softened? What do you see differently now? Write down everything that came up for you.

When money becomes a character, it's easy to see how much power we've given it in our stories. The good news? We can take back that power, become the author and rewrite the role money plays, making a supporting character without any lines.

Next, we'll look at the broader themes money brings into our lives – the beliefs and patterns that shape to plot.

Chapter 4
Themes

"Greed, for lack of a better word, is good."
—Gordon Gekko, *Wall Street*

June 1985

When I walked into the office, I knew I was in trouble. The walls seemed to fold in around me as I walked to my cubicle. Co-workers turned their heads, not wanting to make eye contact. I knew what was coming. I was going to be fired. It was inevitable. Two days earlier, I had told Kevin, my boss, what I thought of him. In all fairness, everyone knew he was an asshole; I was just the only one who said anything about it.

The problem was I would be out of work. The work I wouldn't miss—it bored me to tears. I was a glorified paper pusher with a fancy title: Account Executive. My clients loved me because I wasn't a typical salesperson—okay, Account Executive. I told the truth and didn't use sales-speak or techno-speak to try to impress anyone with my brilliance. As a result, if I said they needed something, they believed me. I wouldn't say it if it wasn't true. And that was the truth. I'm a great storyteller, but I can't say something will help you if I don't believe it will.

I would, however, miss the paycheck. This was my pattern. I'd work at a job that paid me well but stole my soul. Then I'd do something to sabotage myself and end up unemployed. I would try to find something that I'd love to do, but that never worked for me. How could I get someone to pay me a ton of money to just speak my mind? I didn't have a clue.

I'm sure the powers that be had spent the last two days speaking with my accounts to let them know I was moving on. That's why they didn't call me in for this meeting until now. I braced myself for the walk to Kevin's office and was shocked to find Kevin and his boss, Marty, waiting for me. Marty never came to this office. I must have really pissed them off.

"Take a seat, Carrie." Just like Marty, straight to the point. I sat. Marty looked distressed. I always liked Marty and didn't like seeing him troubled. Why he came to fire me was beyond the pale and reminded me why I thought Kevin was a jerk: he needed his boss to do his dirty work.

I didn't think. I didn't have anything planned. I just spoke. "Marty, I was coming in today to say that I'm going to leave. I don't think I can work here any longer. It's just not for me."

Marty's face went from distress to relief. It's not fun firing someone, so I could give him that. I went a step further. "I can give you a two-week notice to give you time to transition my clients, or I can leave now." I was surprised at how calm I felt, as if I were fulfilling something preordained.

Marty smiled and said, "If you leave today, we can say you were let go. That way, you can collect unemployment. It's not much, but it can help while you look elsewhere. I assume you don't have anything else lined up."

He was right about that. And he was right that unemployment wasn't much—about a quarter of my weekly take-home pay. But with that and my limited savings, I was covered for a few weeks. I had no idea what I would do. What I wanted to do was even more unclear. But at least I was away from that horrible environment. I was free.

Themes

What I discovered was that behind the surface patterns of these stories was a theme, an ongoing thread that quietly reinforced my limited relationship with abundance and, most interestingly, with money. In my story above, the theme was constant movement: jumping from job to job, always stressing about where the next paycheck would come from. It didn't matter whether I was happy (I wasn't) or fulfilled. I would upend my life chasing after a sense of financial security. The bigger the paycheck, the better. Eventually, the pattern became so familiar that I left traditional employment altogether and became a consultant/freelancer/1099 contractor. It gave me freedom and spared me from the corporate politics I never fit into. But it also kept the pattern alive. I could walk away from any contract at any time, still looking for the secret to abundance that always seemed just out of reach.

The theme to any story is the overarching drive, the central idea the story is exploring. It's the reason you're telling this particular story rather than any other. The theme is examined through elements like plot and conflict that bring the notion into focus. Characters and language embody the theme. When you watch a movie or read a book, the authors want you to walk away having learned something about life. Common examples of story themes include good versus evil, survival at all costs, love and all its meanings, coming of age and more.

The same applies to your money stories. When I look at the story I shared above, it was a confirmation of one of my most limiting themes: **"Chasing Money above all else."** I carried this theme far longer than I needed to, but until I acknowledged it and chose a new theme, my story kept repeating the same pattern and the same frustration. Here's the good news: by first acknowledging that it was a theme that I accepted, I gave myself the power to move beyond it. Taking ownership is key.

Working with Themes

Where do your themes originate? They start with the foundational messages you receive. Not every comment from family and friends stays with you. It depends on a few things.

First, what was the emotional state of the person that made the statement? Were they angry, frustrated or scared? An emotional charge gives the words more weight. You also need to consider your own emotional state when you received the message: were you looking for support or relief? Were you trying to make sense of a new situation.

Second, was the comment delivered with authority? Statements from authority figures (parents, teachers, leaders/experts) often land as facts, not to be argued with. And if you're a toddler or child, an authority figure carries even more weight. At that age, you don't yet have the experience or language to challenge what's being said. So you accept it and add it to your repertoire of beliefs to live by.

Putting this together, here's an example of how a theme is born:

My client "Marie" came to see me after she took my introductory Money Rewritten™ course online. She had been feeling taken advantage of at work, on call most evenings and weekends with little or no compensation. She thought I could help her script a request for a raise to cover all the extra time. I suggested that before we came up with an approach, we look at some of her money stories, particularly those with her immediate family.

Marie was the only daughter and the oldest of three children. Her brothers were three and five years younger. Growing up, she was given a lot of responsibility. Her parents gave her chores around the house and tied her allowance to the number of tasks she completed. If she made her bed, she received a certain amount. If she also made her brother's beds, she's got an additional dollar or two. Same with the dishes and general housework. Her brothers didn't do any housekeeping. As infants and toddlers, Marie was often told to "keep an eye on her brothers" if her parents left the room. By the time she was twelve, she was their babysitter when her parents went out, earning a small increase in her allowance.

Sometimes when she was home alone with them, they acted out, especially her middle brother. He resented having to listen to his sister, who was only a couple of years older. He'd refuse to go to bed and would keep playing his video games. No matter what Marie said, he ignored her until he heard his parents' car in the driveway, then he'd run to bed. If he was tired the next day or his homework wasn't done, he'd find a way to pin it on Marie. When that happened, Marie's parents deducted money from her allowance. When Marie became frustrated and said she didn't want to babysit anymore, her mother told her that it was her job as the eldest. When Marie asked to be paid more, her mother scoffed, saying she had new clothes and many things most people didn't have.

Meanwhile, Marie's brothers received a set allowance that wasn't tied to chores. Every week they got the same amount.

Marie accepted her situation. After all, it was what she knew. She went on to college and got a degree in computer science. She left her first job after three years when she discovered that, even with more experience and responsibilities, she made less than the other team members. At her current job (the one she came to see me about), she wanted help scripting her raise. I pointed out that, in our sessions, we uncovered a pattern: working harder and taking on more responsibilities, often others' tasks, yet getting paid less. Her theme, she discovered, was that she had to carry the weight of the people around her. Starting with her family and continuing to her first job out or college, she also identified instances in high school and college where she carried the load for classmates and sorority sisters.

It opened her eyes to the patterns and, in doing so, loosened its unconscious hold. Armed with this awareness, she knew exactly what to say to her manager and got her raise. She also prepared a fair on-call rotation for the team that everyone accepted.

In Marie's case, her theme began with her mother tying her allowance to the work she did and then giving Marie more tasks without an increase in compensation. Being the first born she was expected to take on more responsibilities. Teachers repeatedly gave her extra to do. Her theme of "I do more for less" – commonly referred to as over-responsibility – took root.

You have your own patterns and themes. That's the beauty of this process. Your theme is yours and you can change it. Let's keep exploring this essential aspect of your money story.

The Plot Thickens

There are a few money themes that are common to a great many people:

- **Scarcity/Lack:** There is never enough, or not enough to go around. The key word here is enough. If you find your inner dialogue revolves around "having enough," chances are you're in scarcity.
- **Worth/Value:** Human beings are born worthy, yet somewhere along the way, you've been told that you're unworthy and undeserving. Some cultures, social settings and even religions reinforce this. You might even believe your bank account is a direct measurement of your worth.
- **Abundance:** Seeing money for what it is: an energy that flows in and out, rather than something to cling to.
- **Power/Control:** Using their money to exert control over people or situations. Employees may feel like they are expected to follow what the boss says "or else." The "my way or the highway" mentality and builds the false narrative that money equals authority.
- **Security/Safety:** You want to feel safe and secure; money is a part of that equation. You need to have the resources for a great life and be prepared for anything that comes up. The challenge is going over the edge, becoming afraid to spend on anything and living in constant anxiety or fear. Aim for a proportional response to this need.
- **Generosity/Obligation:** Having resources can create a sense of obligation to give to anyone who asks. The goal is to strike a balance between the level of altruism that feels right for you before you give everything away to avoid guilt.

- **Guilt/Shame:** This theme threads through many others. You may believe "wanting money makes me greedy or selfish," or feel shame for not having enough, especially at times of need or when you want something important.
- **Struggle/Earn:** You've been taught that working hard is noble. Stories of people who climb their way to the top through years of effort and struggle are celebrated, while those whose life comes easily are quietly judged. You're told she was born with a "silver spoon" because her life looks carefree, but beneath that is an unspoken belief that her abundance wasn't earned and therefore isn't deserved.
- **Luck/Fate:** You've heard the phrase "being in the right place at the right time," as if luck or fate decides who succeeds. That can make it easy to downplay your own power and choices. But luck and fate aren't the enemy — they're often the quiet partners that meet you halfway when you start rewriting your money story and taking aligned, inspired action.

You may see yourself in more than one theme and that's okay. Many of us have multiple themes around money. You might be generous because you feel guilty about the abundance you enjoy. Or you might seek abundance while carrying the theme "rich people are greedy or immoral." Conflicting themes can paralyze you and keep you stuck. The work is to identify your particular patterns and name the money themes at play.

Once identified, themes lose their hidden power. You can move forward with clarity and purpose instead of living on autopilot. It's empowering.

Plot Points

To recap:

- Themes are the main belief that holds your money story in place.

- You can have multiple themes running simultaneously.

- Conflicting themes can paralyze you and keep you stuck in old patterns.

- Identifying themes brings them out of the shadows and gives you the opportunity to change them.

What's Your Story

So how do you work with themes? As always the first step is to uncover the themes operating in your life. Use these steps to help you determine them:

Step 1: Think of your most common, repeated money struggle. For example, do you worry about overspending? Do you feel guilty that you make more money than someone you know? Do you downplay your financial situation? These are clues to your theme.

Step 2: List any conflicting themes you hold. Most of you have at least one.

Step 3: Think about your money language. I'll review this in greater detail in a later chapter, but for these purposes, the words you use when discussing money or finances are clues. Do you talk about what you can or can't afford? Do you struggle with "never having enough"? Do you believe working hard and earning a paycheck is a more than a necessity, it's a noble endeavor? Do you live "paycheck to paycheck" or struggle to "make ends meet"? When you think about these phrases, how does your body respond? Do you get a knot in your stomach? A sinking feeling?

Step 4: Take what you've noted in the previous steps and give your money story a title. It could be: "Another Day Another Dollar" or "Out of the Woods" or "Roll the Dice." It can be clever or on-the-nose. Take your time and see what comes up. This is your money story and bringing it to light makes it easier to change.

These themes show you why change can feel impossible. The story held in place by these themes has been running for years. But here's the truth: you can't change something you're not aware of. When you discover this pattern, own it. Owning it gives you the power to shift the narrative. You'll find that when you do this exercise, transformation can happen as quickly as you're ready for it.

Next, I'll show you the avenues from which you allow money to enter your life. It's an eye-opening experience.

Chapter 5
Avenues of Receiving Money

"You make your own luck."
—Eddie Felson, *The Hustler*

July 1991

I sat in my apartment in Avon Connecticut, bemoaning my terrible life. I didn't understand why things never seemed to go my way. I graduated from Penn State, worked at crappy jobs that I hated but paid me well, I even got a huge pile of money when AT&T transferred me here.

I'd been with them five miserable years, but the income was stable and I even vested my retirement plan before I left to move to England. Only I didn't go to the University of London as I planned. I wanted a bona fide degree in English Literature – where better to do that than in the United Kingdon? I sold my condo and made enough to cover my expenses in London for the year-long program.

Then Mom died, and I felt so guilty that I didn't go. Tessa and I sold Mom's home and shared the proceeds leaving me with another $20,000 to go with the money I had left from my condo.

So what did I do? I opened a jewelry store with a friend because that's what you do when you have no retail experience and more money than you ever had burning a hole in your bank account. I hated all that money; I had to spend it. Besides, the jewelry story would make me rich and then I'd be set for life.

The store failed and even after selling all the inventory I barely paid off the vendors who supplied the products for the store. Around that time, another friend told me she'd won some money in the lottery. It wasn't much, but it was enough to keep her buying tick-ets. When she suggested it to me, I was appalled. My parents were gamblers, and I swore as a child that I would never gamble in any form. I didn't even buy scratchers, which were just gaining popular-ity then.

I called someone I knew from AT&T. He was working with a new technology company and immediately offered me a job that paid double what I made at AT&T. I didn't think; I just accepted.

And now here I sit. Another crappy job that pays well, and I just want to cut my wrists. Would I ever figure out a way to have enough money so that I wouldn't have to keep living like this?

Writing the story I shared brought up a great deal of sadness for the person I was in 1991. I thought the only way to have money was to work at jobs I hate, just like Mom and Dad. I know they both relied on the income they got from gambling, but that left such a bad taste in my mouth that I couldn't bring myself to ever try. I judged them for gambling even though my dad made enough to keep the family afloat. And then, when I was twelve, Dad won the lottery. It was enough to pay off our house. He even gave each of us fifty dollars. I remember my eyes growing wide as I held that money in my hands. I felt a rush of energy. I understood, in my young mind, why Dad gambled. It was intoxicating and scary all at once. Even so, I still didn't trust relying on luck as a financial plan.

Most of you have one or two possible ways money can come in. These are the avenues you were taught to believe in. Anything outside of them feels impossible or even wrong. When faced with a new way of receiving money – an inheritance or gift for example – you might feel uncomfortable or anxious. When this happens, listen to what your body is telling you. You're about to step outside your normal pattern of receiving money.

Money Avenues

I define Money Avenues as the pathways you believe money can legitimately and reliably flow into your life. The most common of these is the employment paycheck. I would venture a guess that over 90% of the population has received a paycheck at some point in their life. Whether it's your first job in high school or college or when you enter the workforce, the paycheck is presumed to be the most stable source of income.

This isn't always the case, as industries change and businesses shift. The pandemic proved that when many businesses shuttered, leaving millions unemployed and forcing people to seek other avenues such as passive income and side hustles.

But how did Money Avenues develop? Families, cultures and societies created acceptable means for the work done and the ways money was received. Over time, these ideas became entrenched, defining what was acceptable and what was to be avoided at all costs. (Pun intended.)

Money Avenues can also be gender and culturally specific. Some cultures believe that women's source of income should come from her father or spouse. Women are often seen in supporting roles such as housekeeping or nursing, although that is changing every day.

I remember the first time I walked into my nail salon, and a man did my manicure. He did one of the best jobs ever, but my first reaction was one of discomfort. It's not often you see men in that role, but more telling was my visceral response.

The point is, when looking at your money story, knowing the avenues for receiving money – and your reaction to them – is an important piece of information to be explored.

So what are some other money avenues?

- **Employment Paycheck** – The most common and acceptable

- **Self-employment/entrepreneurship** – Closely related to regular employment but you often feel more ownership in your work and value around the money you receive

- **Savings/investments** – Interest, dividends, stocks, retirement accounts

- **Loans/credit cards** – Credit cards, car loans, school loans or mortgage.

- **Side Hustles** – Second jobs, tutoring, driving for Uber/Lyft

- **Passive income** – Rental income, royalties, licensing or affiliate earnings.

- **Family/Gifts** – Inheritance, gifts, or income from a spouse or partner.

- **Luck** – Lottery, Sweepstakes, Gambling

- **Windfall/Bonuses** – Unexpected surprises

- **Community/Crowdfunding** – GoFundMe, grants, donations

- **Government Benefits** – Disability, social security, unemployment

- **Lawsuits/Settlements** – Legal awards or insurance payouts

- **Other** – What unique ways do you bring money into your life?

The Impact of Limited Money Avenues

Now that we've explored the various Money Avenues, let's look at how you relate to them — and the emotions that come with each one. These insights give you a clearer, more complete picture of your relationship with money.

If you believe the only way to receive money is through a paycheck, you've probably shut down other ways for it to flow into your life. You may have been taught that a paycheck is the most respectable or stable method, and that anything else feels risky or "not for you." Over time, that belief can make you feel stuck with your "lot in life" or resigned to one limited path of earning.

Many of you are entrepreneurs or self-employed in some capacity. While that can feel riskier, it also offers a stronger sense of control, creativity, and purpose. Still, some of you may feel one client away from being broke. My self-employed clients often tell me they sleep better when they have a backup plan and a savings cushion to carry them through slow cycles.

Most of you have a savings account or some kind of retirement plan. But have you looked at other options for growth? Investments in the stock or bond markets, for example, can open new avenues for receiving. Certificates of Deposit (CDs) are another simple option — some start at just $100 — and they typically offer higher interest rates, though your funds are locked until maturity.

Some of you may be ready to invest in real estate. Real estate can open doors to passive income and valuable tax advantages. Don't let news reports about the difficulty of buying property discourage you. There are new, creative ways people are joining forces and pooling resources to purchase together. And there's no shortage of online tools and communities to help you learn what's possible. If you've told yourself that investing "isn't for you," take another look at that belief. Where did it come from, and can you begin to shift it? Investing can be one of the most rewarding and empowering Money Avenues when approached with curiosity and care.

Almost everyone carries some kind of loan — credit cards, student loans, a mortgage, or a car payment. The key is to use credit as a tool, not a long-term plan. I once had a client who lived entirely on credit cards. She was buried in debt and had to take some tough steps to climb out. This isn't a judgment, it's a reminder: stay aware, stay intentional, and make sure you're in charge of your debt before it takes charge of you.

Luck can be a tricky money avenue. It's exciting, unpredictable, and full of possibility — and that's exactly why it can pull us in so easily. I once worked with a client who believed that luck was her only way out. She spent hours entering sweepstakes, buying scratch-offs, and checking horoscopes for "lucky days." For her, it wasn't about the game itself — it was about the hope. The idea that one lucky break could erase years of struggle.

The truth is, luck isn't a strategy; it's a visitor. It might stop by, but it doesn't often stay. Depending on it too much takes up the space where a strong relationship with money — one built on intention and trust — could reside. Serendipity, however, is different. Serendipity shows up when you're present, aware, and open to possibility. It isn't forced, and it doesn't come from desperation. It happens when your mindset and actions align, and opportunities naturally begin to appear — a new client calls, a refund arrives, someone introduces you to a connection you didn't even know you needed.

That's not random luck. That's flow. And the more grounded you are in your worth, the more serendipity has room to find you.

What about side hustles? Many of you may have driven for Uber or Lyft to make extra cash. I know several people who, every year around the holidays, pick up additional shifts or take on short-term seasonal work. There are so many creative ways to bring in "extra" money. You might tutor or teach a skill you've developed from one of your hobbies — music, writing, or a favorite craft. Make it something you enjoy sharing and let it be okay that you're paid for your time. Remember, money is simply an exchange of value for value, so be comfortable with that.

One of my clients, an account executive at a major corporation, loved to travel. She could easily fly somewhere every weekend if she had the chance. She lived near her local airport, and one evening, after returning from a trip, she stopped at the ticket counter of her favorite airline. On a whim, she asked if they had any part-time or evening work available, knowing employees often received great travel perks. They did — and she was hired for three evening shifts a week at the ticket counter. She loved the extra money, but even more, the travel benefits allowed her to explore new destinations two or three times a month.

Another client started a small online shop selling her hand-made jewelry. What began as a creative outlet quickly became a reliable source of additional income. She told me the biggest shift wasn't just in her bank account — it was in how she saw herself. For the first time, she felt confident charging for her creativity and proud that her art could bring joy to others. That confidence opened new doors she hadn't even considered before.

Whether your side hustle is practical or passion-driven, it serves a bigger purpose than the money it brings in. It builds confidence, reminds you that you can create opportunities, and strengthens your belief that abundance flows from your own ideas and effort.

I mentioned passive income earlier when talking about real estate, but there are many other ways to bring in money without spending time for what you earn. Passive income can come from licensing your intellectual property, earning royalties from a book or a piece of music, selling an online course, or even creating content on a YouTube channel. If you have specific skills or knowledge, you can share them through these platforms and get paid for the value you provide. The beauty of passive income is that once the initial work is done, it can continue to generate money with far less effort, giving you more freedom to focus on what you love.

Families are another potential source of money. If you're in a relationship, your spouse or partner often shares in household expenses, helping with your monthly financial responsibilities. Some of you may also receive an inheritance or regular monetary gifts from family. An inheritance is usually a one-time event, but when it happens, it can be an incredible boost. It falls into what I call the "windfall avenue" — those moments when unexpected money flows into your life.

Windfalls can take many forms. You might receive an end-of-year bonus, a signing bonus when you start a new job, a relocation package from your company, or even a payout from your landlord if they need you to move out of a rental early. For those who work internationally, there can be overseas stipends or housing allowances that ease the transition to another country. Even an unexpected tax refund falls into this category. These moments often overlap with other money avenues and serve as powerful reminders that money can show up in more ways than you've been taught to expect.

Community and crowdfunding options often arise during times of great need. You might reach out to your network of friends, family, or colleagues for help with a personal project, a medical challenge, or another situation that requires a quick cash infusion. Crowdfunding can be a powerful way to grow support, but to do it well takes time, energy, and planning. I suggest reaching out to a service or expert who can help you set up your campaign. They can save you from common missteps and may even help you tap into their networks to widen your reach.

Many people feel shame when they find themselves in need of support, or they judge others who rely on assistance from government programs. But help exists for a reason. Think back to what happened during the pandemic — without PPP loans and other relief programs, millions would have faced devastating losses of income, housing, and food security. Yes, there were abuses, but that doesn't erase the lives that were stabilized because help was available. If you lose your job after a company merger or find yourself suddenly unemployed, collecting benefits while you find your next opportunity isn't weakness — it's wisdom. It keeps you out of panic and buys you the stability to make better long-term choices.

The same is true for lawsuits and settlements. While there will always be people who take advantage of the system, there's also legitimate need. If you're injured and unable to work for a period of time, disability insurance can be a lifeline. If you receive a settlement from a situation that caused you harm, that money serves as temporary relief while you get back on your feet. The key in all of these cases is to find balance — to accept help without guilt, use it wisely, and trust that these resources exist to support you when you need them most.

The goal here isn't to try every possible avenue for bringing in money. It's to expand your awareness — to open yourself to the idea that money can flow in from many different sources, some you may never have considered before. As we'll explore in the upcoming chapter, this awareness is what helps you raise your money ceiling and create a life where abundance feels natural, supported, and steady.

The Plot Thickens

As I was writing this chapter, I had an immediate insight. I've been building my *Rewritten Collection*™ into a full business — courses, books, masterclasses — and as I reviewed my budget, one of my first thoughts for funding was to take out a second mortgage. It was a familiar, seductive idea. We had plenty of equity, but was adding another mortgage really wise?

That thought took me back years earlier, to a time when I was so uncomfortable with money that I rushed to spend it on a doomed business just to get rid of it. Now, standing in a very different place, I saw the pattern for what it was — that old reflex to undermine what I'd built. Our home had gained real value, the result of years of work and stability. Did I really want to risk that now?

Around that same time, I was talking with a filmmaker friend who said something that stopped me cold. "I never use my own money to fund projects," he said. "Investors." It struck me immediately — this was an avenue I'd never even considered. Another door opening, another belief shifting.

At this point, you might be wondering how you'll know when you've begun opening to new avenues for receiving money. The truth is, it can happen in surprising or subtle ways.

One person in one of my introductory courses believed money only came through struggle and hard work. That belief was deeply rooted in religion — "the meek shall inherit the earth." Even after leaving that upbringing behind, the belief was still there, running quietly in the background. Two days after the workshop, they emailed me: they'd been offered a new job with better hours and more pay. That's how quickly change can begin to show itself.

Sometimes the signs are smaller but just as meaningful. You might receive an unexpected gift, a new client "out of the blue," or a small windfall that catches you off guard. One client started receiving credit card offers with zero interest for several months — something she'd never qualified for before. Another was given a scratch-off lottery ticket as a thank-you and won twenty-five dollars. Not a life-changing amount, but enough to show that something was moving, shifting, realigning.

The point is to pay attention. Notice these small but powerful moments. Celebrate them. Every single one is a sign that a transformation is underway — that your money story is beginning to open, and your life is responding in kind.

Plot Points

To recap:

- Money Avenues give you a clearer view of your relationship with money.

- Start by exploring your current comfort zone for receiving money and what that means for you.

- Expect emotions and judgments to surface as you do this work; they're part of the process.

- Keeping a list of the signs or indications that show your progress.

- Even the smallest changes are worth celebrating.

- You're breaking old patterns. Give yourself the time and patience you deserve.

What's Your Story

What are some steps you can take to uncover your money avenues?

Step 1: To create lasting change, you first need to know where you are right now. List the ways you currently allow money into your world. If you're unsure, think about how money flowed in your family. Note any emotions, judgments, or memories that arise.

Step 2: How do you feel about the money avenues you don't use? Do you judge or avoid them? For example, does inheritance feel unfair? Does the lottery feel like cheating? Do some options feel off-limits — and why?

Step 3: Imagine adding a new avenue you've never considered. Notice what feelings come up.

Step 4: Imagine receiving money in a new and surprising way. Create a scene where it happens. Write or draw what you see. How does it feel — both the receiving and the imagining?

These exercises open the pathways for receiving money in your life.

Most people stay on the same familiar money streets, repeating the same patterns. You can explore new possibilities and expand the opportunities available to you. It's within you.

In the next chapter, we'll look at the language of money — the words you use that keep you on those familiar, limited pathways for receiving.

Chapter 6
The Language of Money

"Words are our most inexhaustible source of magic."
—**Albus Dumbledore,** *Harry Potter and the Deathly Hallows Part 2*

May 2004

Walking through Bloomingdale's in the Century City Mall was one of my favorite pastimes. I loved looking at all the beautiful clothes I'd never afford. The shoes were a particular favorite, but who pays $1,900 for boots? Granted, they were gorgeous, and the leather was as soft and pliable as a well-worn glove. The handbags were divine. The jewelry was impressive. They had a large number of suede leather coats, some spectacular sherpas that made me wonder what they were doing in Los Angeles. Probably for all the skiing trips the clientele took to Aspen or Switzerland—trips I'd never take.

I had to work for a living. I couldn't go jetting off on a whim, and I certainly couldn't buy that gorgeous sheepskin parka that must have felt like heaven when worn. All this stuff was too expensive, so far out of my budget it would take a telescope to see it. I'm sure these never go on sale. I wonder if there are any bargain suede coats.

Tessa liked to say that she was frugal and always looked for things that were on sale or inexpensive. I didn't share her views. I was so ashamed that Mom shopped at Target, buying cheap, ugly clothes that never fit her well. They either hung poorly or were too tight in the wrong places. It was embarrassing. I promised myself I'd never buy my clothes at Target, but it didn't look like Bloomingdale's would be my go-to store either.

So I window-shopped and dreamed and wondered what it would be like to own a $2,000 handbag or an $800 cashmere scarf. Maybe someday, but definitely not today. I couldn't afford it.

The Words We Use

As I was writing this story, I realized something important. Without any other point of reference, I had accepted this view of money as fact. In truth, it was simply a reflection of my family's belief in scarcity, the idea that "lack" was a normal part of life. I grew up thinking that money wasn't about numbers or exchange or value; it was about survival. In my family story, money had taken the starring role, and I had unknowingly adopted the script.

Through repetition, that language became part of me. Writing the opening scene brought that truth home. It shaped what I thought, how I felt, and every decision I made about money. I lived by the belief that "making ends meet" and "working hard at any job I could get" weren't just expectations, they were badges of honor.

I remember coming home from my part-time job as a cashier in high school. My boss told me how impressed she was with my work and said that when I graduated, she hoped I'd consider taking a full-time position as head cashier. She even mentioned that I could work my way up to store manager. She meant it as a compliment, a sign of respect.

But my stomach turned. And when I told my mom, she was thrilled. I reminded her that I wanted to go to college. From there, it went downhill fast. Mom told me I was foolish, living in a fantasy. "You're throwing your life away when you could have a good paycheck and benefits," she said. "How else will you support yourself?"

That was my mother's worldview — and by extension, mine. For as long as I can remember, her comments centered on how hard it was to have enough to live an "okay" life. She couldn't even entertain the idea of abundance. In her eyes, our family would never be more than who we already were: lower-class people in a middle-class world.

When my older sister, Sally, landed a job in television and started making real money, she celebrated by buying Dad a new stereo and some of his favorite albums. She shopped in an upscale boutique in Oakmont, a wealthier neighborhood not far from our home in Verona. Mom's reaction was cutting: "Sally's showing off." To her, even nice clothes couldn't erase the working-class blood running through our veins.

The Power of Money Language

The words we use around money reveal the stories we carry. Maybe you've said, "I can't afford it," or "It's so expensive," or been told to "live within your means." These phrases may sound harmless, but they point to something deeper — a relationship with money that needs attention.

The language you use gives enormous weight to the role money plays in your life. It can reinforce limitations and keep you locked under a low money ceiling. Your money ceiling represents the maximum amount of money you're comfortable having in your life. It's built from your inherited stories, your sense of identity and worth, your emotions, and the cultural messages you've absorbed over time.

When you're ready to raise that ceiling, start with your language. The words you speak are the first bricks you can remove — one phrase, one belief at a time.

The Plot Thickens

The words you use around money are often the clearest evidence of the stories you carry and the relationship you have with money itself. Words like *afford, bargain, cheap, wasteful, not enough to go around,* are just a few examples of limiting words that keep you stuck in scarcity, lack and struggle.

If you were told to "live within your means" it's time to look and see whether that belief still belongs in your identity.

Words matter. Language is how your brain encodes your beliefs, and beliefs are the guiding mantras of your life. The repetition and daily examples drive these notions deep into your being. They become the emotional wiring that stays with you operating undetected until you bring it forward and address it.

If you believe there's "not enough to go around" you're dealing with a scarcity mentality. In economics, this is called the "zero sum game." It means that if there is only a limited supply of something, once it's gone, it's gone. If you have twenty dollars and say a thief steals it from you. The thief has twenty dollars, and you have zero.

Money is a construct. More of it is created all the time, yet our beliefs – revealed through our language – tells us that there is only a limited amount to go around. With that mindset, every time you hear about billionaires accumulating more wealth, you may subconsciously believe there's less for everyone else. That premise is completely false.

What about phrases such as "that's too expensive," "don't be greedy," or "it must be nice that they can…," or "they're selfish"? This phrasing shows that you're carrying shame around money. If you associate shame with abundance you won't be happy with your success.

One of my clients finally bought the car of her dreams – a Tesla. She was thrilled, but she refused to tell her family because she didn't want them to "rain on her parade and crush her dreams." I was heartbroken for her. The people who should have supported her did not. But it was also an opportunity to see her money script and, armed with this awareness, change it.

Scarcity and shame are just two examples of how language shapes how you function and interact with money and abundance. It dictates your spending habits, reflects your sense of self-worth, and determines how much you're willing to take risks. Most importantly, it affects your ability to receive.

If you've ever downplayed a gift, a windfall or even the abundance you currently enjoy, you are in a dysfunctional relationship with money.

The good news is, you can change it. The even better news is that language is everywhere. Because of that, you can get immediate results.

Most languages are nuanced and carry words with shades of meanings. Here's one example, I advised a client to change a single phrase in her life. She had a habit of saying that she bought something that was "cheap." I suggested she use the word "inexpensive" instead. "Cheap" implied low cost, but also low quality or poor taste. "Inexpensive," on the other hand, suggested discernment and a smart thoughtful purchase.

She made the change and almost immediately, her approach to money shifted. She became more thoughtful about what she bought and more confident about the value it brought her.

The goal isn't to become overly positive, or what some call "toxic positivity." It's to take back your power through awareness and choice.

Plot Points

To recap:

- The words you use reveal your relationship with money.

- Money language, developed through years of repetition and experience, determines your beliefs and emotional wiring.

- You can change your language immediately with significant results.

What's Your Story

Step 1: List three money phrases you remember hearing growing up. What was the setting and who said them? How often were they repeated and by whom?

Step 2: Write down three money phrases you use now without thinking. Bringing them forward is the first step in changing your language.

Step 3: Do you recall where you first heard these phrases? Who said them?

Step 4: How do these phrases make you feel in your body when you say or hear them? Does your stomach churn? Do you feel proud or small? What other feelings come up?

Step 5: Choose one phrase and rewrite it in your own words — something that feels true but more expansive. For example, instead of "I can't afford that" try "I'm considering where this fits right now." Instead of "It must be nice that they can afford a new car every year," think "That is inspiring and shows me what's possible."

The words you use around money are one of the strongest indicators of your relationship with money and abundance. Start by changing the language and you'll begin notice how your story changes.

But language isn't the only force at play. Sometimes, the biggest shifts come when crisis lands on your doorstep. These moments test your money stories and push us to change.

Chapter 7
Challenges, Crises
& Conflict

"Hardest time of your life? That's when you find out who you really are. —**Creed, *Rocky Balboa***

April 1998

I showed up on set at my regular call time. We were wrapping up a commercial and this was the last day of filming. I still had a few more days of work ahead of me to complete paperwork and make sure all the costumes, props and equipment were returned to the rental companies. After that, I wanted to talk to Bruce, the director, and Mason, his producer, about the next project and when I'd report for work. Once I knew, I planned to take a much-needed break to visit Tessa in Northern California.

The production office was quiet, which wasn't surprising since I came in an hour before most of the other crew. I knew Mason was around somewhere, and so I went straight to my computer and prepped for the day. Mason walked in just as I was finishing my work.

"Good. You're here." Mason sounded chipper, which wasn't something I would normally associate with her. She could be moody and brooding, but this had been a tough shoot with all the night scenes.

"Yes! I'm ready for today and have all that I need to wrap this one. When you get a chance, I'd love to talk to you about my schedule for the next project." I tried to match her upbeat tone. I'd read somewhere that mirroring people's energy helps connection.

"The thing is, after today, we won't need you any longer, Carrie."

Again, chipper. Too chipper. It didn't make sense.

"Why? Who's going to handle the returns and the paperwork? What about Bruce's next project? It starts in two weeks!" My voice cracked. I sounded as shocked and scared as I felt.

"I've got everything I need to wrap this one. We won't need you for the next. So you can take as long a break as you like."

Her words landed like a slap. Mason handed me my last paycheck. This was planned. She'd known all along she was letting me go today. I had no time to prepare, no chance to line up another gig. I was well and truly screwed.

The check covered rent and a couple of bills, but that was it. I drove to Tessa's and stayed with her for a while, trying to process the fear and disbelief swirling through me.

What was I going to do?

The Message in the Meltdown

It's one thing to talk about money when things are going well. But the real stories, the ones that show your deepest beliefs, come out in times of crisis.

If you think about the protagonist in any movie, she's tested by challenge after challenge, each one raising the tension until she reaches the breaking point. Then comes the turning point, the moment of truth, when the decision to grow becomes clear. That's how it works in real life, too.

Crises and challenges force you to face yourself. They show you where your energy needs to go so real change can begin. They aren't obstacles to avoid but essential defining moments that ensure you get the message and make the shift you've been resisting.

Crises expose your hidden narrative. Do you secretly believe there isn't enough to go around, or that you don't deserve an easy relationship with money? What story do you tell yourself in moments of crisis?

They're not punishments. They're wake-up calls.

Shandy's Story

A friend of mine had a major ordeal with her bank. Someone accessed her savings account and stole several thousand dollars. The bank eventually recovered the money and, as a precaution, changed everything: her login ID, passwords, and security questions. They closed the old account and opened a new one. A week later, it happened again—and this time they took double.

After much back and forth, the bank recovered the funds but froze Shandy's accounts. When she called, they asked her a series of questions to verify her identity. After fifteen minutes of questions and texted verification codes, it was determined that she could not access her accounts. She was locked out of her money completely.

Shandy called me in tears. "That's all my life savings. What am I going to do?"

Her fear poured through the phone. After she took a few calming breaths, we talked. It took time, but what came out was powerful. Shandy uncovered deeply rooted emotions around money. Beneath her anger and panic, she found a lifelong belief: if she had money, she'd lose it; she couldn't be trusted with it; it wasn't safe.

She realized she had been holding money in a viselike grip—afraid to spend it, afraid to move it, afraid to enjoy it. She had been holding money captive, thinking it gave her security and peace.

When Shandy finally relaxed that grip and began managing money from a place of worth and value, everything shifted. Within months, money began to flow freely. She had more clients and her savings nearly doubled.

In that single crisis, she uncovered most of her story—and the root of her stressful relationship with money.

That's what crisis does. It exposes beliefs and brings buried fears to the surface. When you face a challenge or crisis, look for the message inside the drama. It may be uncomfortable, but if you listen, it shows you the way through.

Crises That Trigger Old Money Scripts

Certain events have a way of shaking the foundation of your money scripts. They hit your most sensitive beliefs about safety, value and control. Some of the most common are:

Changes in Employment – Losing a job or work contract brings up fears about stability and self-worth. It doesn't matter if you loved your job or were already planning to leave. The change rattles your sense of identity, confidence and self-esteem.

Debt – Loans and credit cards create constant pressure that can feed guilt and shame mixed with anxiety, locking you into the same cycle you're trying to escape.

Unexpected Expenses – There was a time when every time I got a bonus or unexpected windfall, something major would break. I'd tell myself "easy come easy go." That belief made it nearly impossible to build saving. Unexpected expenses can arise at any time. If you're not prepared with some savings or a plan to respond, they can spark anxiety and trigger fight-or-flight reaction that make it harder to think clearly and find your way through.

Who Am I to Deserve This – When new opportunities show up, many of you shrink back. That inner voice questioning your right to have more? That's a money story about your worthiness. Sit with it. Ask who's speaking. It's a powerful chance to shift your relationship with money.

Crises and challenges don't just test you; they push right up against the edges of what you believe is possible. A crisis reveals your wounds, and once you can see them, you know exactly where you need to focus. From there, you can heal and start expanding your relationship with money.

The Plot Thickens

Money is one of the most common sources of tension in relationships, families, and even within yourself. It touches nearly every part of life. When beliefs or expectations clash, emotions can run high.

Here are a few all-too-familiar examples:

- Are parents obligated to buy cars or pay for college for all their children? What if one child wants to travel instead?

- The tradition of the father of the bride paying for the wedding has shifted, yet I've seen families split apart when one daughter wanted her father to pay and another thought that was unfair, especially since she wasn't planning to marry.

- Inheritance disputes can be some of the most painful, especially in blended families. I've found that the larger the amount of money involved, the greater the emotional fallout.

Each of these examples exposes deep feelings of fairness, entitlement, and expectation. They reveal hidden money stories—assumptions about what "should" happen with family money. When reality doesn't match those expectations, emotions like anger, guilt, and resentment surface quickly.

These moments matter. They show where your stories conflict and where your relationship with money needs attention. Whether you're the parent making financial choices or the son or daughter questioning them, these situations are opportunities to step back, see the narrative at play, and create a healthier perspective.

Crises like these aren't proof that you're broken or incapable of change. In truth, they reveal what stands between you and true financial freedom. The emotions that arise in conflict are invitations to heal. When you face them with awareness instead of avoidance, you begin to rebuild a relationship with money that supports peace, not stress.

As a friend once said, "The breakdown points to the breakthrough."

Money Warning Signs™: When Money Takes on a Deeper Meaning

Crises and challenges often start small, a disagreement, a bill, a sudden change, but they point to something deeper: a story that's ready to be rewritten. Sometimes those stories show up in predictable moments, the kind that touch every life at one time or another. I call these Money Warning Signs™ because they highlight the places where your money narrative may be asking for attention, compassion, and change.

Health Crisis: Medical debt can be devastating. Insurance rarely covers the full cost of specialized care, leaving people underinsured and overwhelmed. When this happens, it's not just financial stress. It's an emotional confrontation with your worth, safety and survival. And it can feel terrifying.

Marriage: Marriage can be both joyful and stressful. It's also a major money merger. Differences in beliefs about spending, saving, and debt can test even strong relationships. Honest conversations about money are essential.

Children: The cost of raising a child can reach hundreds of thousands of dollars. It also brings up old beliefs about sacrifice, responsibility and the kind of parent, and provider, you think you "should" be.

Divorce: Separation splits more than finances. It brings up grief, fear, anger and questions about self-worth and security. It can also reveal where your story of dependence or control needs work.

Home Ownership: For many, home ownership represents success and safety. For others, it brings stress about debt, credit, and stability. Both are stories. How you interpret that mortgage or that equity says a great deal about your relationship with security.

College Education: The burden of student loans is one of today's biggest money stressors. It brings up stories of fairness and expectation within families, especially when parents cannot help all children equally.

Decrease in Income: Job loss, business slowdown, or retirement all test your trust in yourself and your ability to rebuild. These moments can feel destabilizing, but they are also invitations to create a new relationship with money.

Plot Points

To recap:

- Crises reveal your hidden narratives, scarcity, self-worth, fears and anxieties.

- Challenges are not bad luck; they are turning points that show what you're ready to shift.

- Every reaction – fear, anger, avoidance – is information. Listen to what it is telling you.

What's Your Story

Step 1: Recall a money crisis you've faced. What story did you tell yourself at the time?

Step 2: What recurring conflicts come up for you (spending, saving, priorities)?

Step 3: What's one crisis you now see as a turning point? What did it reveal?

Challenges and crises aren't there to punish you. They are story catalysts showing you exactly where your old scripts are hiding. Awareness is the first step to lasting change.

In the next chapter we'll learn the process for rewriting your money stories.

Chapter 8
Money Ceiling

"The only thing standing between you and your goal is the story you keep telling yourself." —**Jordan Belfort,**
The Wolf of Wall Street

August 2002

Balancing my checkbook always came with the same dread and the same headache. I'd sit there, imaginary fingers crossed, hoping the math would magically land in my favor. On this day, I was at the table in my Los Angeles apartment. The sky outside was a perfect Southern California blue that makes you feel lucky to live here.

I didn't feel lucky. I felt trapped.

My balance was under a thousand dollars. Again. It didn't matter what I cut back on or how careful I was. After the bills cleared, that number never seemed to move. It was like my bank account had a limit and I kept banging into it every single month.

I started digging through my usual mess of receipts, pay stubs, and unopened envelopes, hoping I'd missed something. Maybe there was a forgotten check hiding in there somewhere. It had happened before, so why not now? But the truth was I didn't have a system. I didn't have a budget. I didn't even know what a "budget" really meant. I just knew I needed one.

And sitting there, looking at that same number staring back at me again, I felt stupid and stuck. I couldn't figure out why I couldn't get ahead no matter how hard I tried. I told myself I wasn't good with money. I told myself other people somehow knew things I didn't. Mostly, I told myself that maybe this was just how my life was going to go.

In that moment, I wondered if a thousand dollars was as far as I was ever going to get.

Money Ceilings

When I look at how I never seemed to be able to break into a higher income bracket or build a real savings account, it comes back to a very clear pattern. It started with my origin story, which included the inherited stories of my early years and the messages from culture and society.

Mom and Dad were both first generation Americans. They brought with them the values and traditions of their respective upbringings. Dad's family was from Italy where women married and became mothers. Mom's family was from Serbia. They were farmers and their gender roles were well defined. Their plan for me was to marry because I needed a man to take care of me. This was not a subtle message hidden in tidy language. From the time I became a teenager, Mom told me that marriage was the best and only option for me.

I was born in the 1950s and grew up in the 1960s and 1970s. The Women's Rights Movement was in full swing, along with a number of other civil and national calls for change. It was the drive for the Equal Rights Amendment, aligned with the Women's Rights Movement, that gave me another view of what it meant to be a woman in the twentieth century.

It also came with a new kind of pressure. I was told that I "should" go after careers traditionally held by men. When I was applying for college, I received more than one call from volunteers telling me that I needed to major in engineering or law to prove that women were as capable as men. It was confusing, not only because it went against everything I was told at home, but because in both scenarios I was never presented an option to discover who I wanted to be. In all the noise of the stories I was hearing, no one showed me how to discover me.

Men had their own challenges and messages. My brother was raised to believe he would be the breadwinner and support his family at any cost. It made him wary of any woman who wanted a career or a life beyond bearing his children. This is not a judgement. It is a reflection on how powerful these messages are and how they shape you into who you become as an adult.

Between my family and the forces in play around us, there was no path to discover my dreams. It was the same for my brother. We were told to follow Mom's and Dad's view of life. It was tempting, because it gave me a sense of belonging to either a family or a cause, but never to myself. How could I find "me" in all that noise.

The confusion stuck with me, ingrained in my psyche and my body. It told me that as a woman there were certain things I could not do. Creating wealth was one of those things. It shaped my personality, my identity and the language I used. Remember, your language is a clear clue as to where you think you fit in and how you see yourself. It reflects where you think you belong.

All of these pieces, your stories, language, identity and emotions, form your Money Ceiling. It is the invisible limit that keeps your level of earning and receiving, and your relationship with money, at a "comfortable" level. Comfortable here is not about joy or fulfillment. It is about familiar. It is the comfort of habit and routine that has wired your brain to stay the person you were yesterday and expect to be tomorrow, unless you make a new choice.

Your Money Ceiling is also tied to your survival needs, held in place by your lizard brain, the old brain that holds you back in the face of perceived danger. Change is seen as dangerous, so you stay comfortable. You cling to belonging that requires a tribe to survive, even though you are well beyond that now. As a human being, you are a social animal. You need contact with others. You fear isolation and so you may give up parts of your authenticity, sacrificing yourself in the process.

All of this becomes the brick and mortar of your ceiling. You may not want to outshine your parents, partners or friends by being more successful or by proving them wrong when you choose a career you love rather than one they selected for you. Instead, you accept the stress and worry and doubt, because the thought of rejection or abandonment feels worse.

To lift the ceiling, or take it down altogether, you must look at each component and take it apart. You have already started that in previous chapters, discovering your stories, your language and the avenues where you are comfortable receiving. These all contribute to your identity. As you dismantle them brick by brick, you become open to greater freedom in all areas of your life.

The Plot Thickens

Money ceilings are not handed to you. They are formed over time. They hold you at a certain level. Your ceiling might be high. It might be low. But you have one. And if you want a healthier relationship with money, knowing what your ceiling is and dismantling it is one of the most important parts of this work.

Your money ceiling is built from many layers. The most common are:

Origin Stories: These are the messages you absorbed from family, culture and society. They are the foundation of your ceiling.

Emotions: Fear, guilt, anxiety, stress, shame. These emotions shape how you relate to wealth and how much ease in having it you allow.

Identity: How do you see yourself with money? Are you someone who takes risks or someone who plays it safe? Identity is one of the strongest forces holding your ceiling in place.

Judgments: Comparing yourself to others creates judgment. Judgment creates stagnation. When you are stuck in judgment, you close the door to financial freedom.

Language: The words you speak and the thoughts you think tell you exactly where your ceiling sits. Language shows itself most clearly during moments of crisis. Pay attention. Your words will reveal your relationship with money.

Self-worth: You were born worthy. Somewhere along the way you may have forgotten that. When self-worth is low, your ceiling stays low.

You often feel the impact of your ceiling in your body before your mind ever catches up. Think back to the times you felt anxious opening a bill, numb when checking your account, or ready to avoid anything involving money. Those reactions are not random. They are clues that you are pushing up against your ceiling.

Your ceiling also shows up when you begin to rise. Sometimes you start earning more than your parents or spouse and a quiet guilt sets in. Other times you receive a bonus or windfall, only to spend it quickly or sabotage the progress. And as I mentioned earlier, these limits often surface during moments of crisis because pressure reveals what you have been holding.

Crises do not just create stress. They expose your thresholds. They show you where your limits live and give you insight into what your ceiling is made of and what needs to shift so you can rise beyond it.

Plot Points

To recap:

- Money Ceilings are the upper limits of the wealth you're willing and able to hold.

- Everyone has a Money Ceiling regardless of how high or low it is.

- Money Ceilings begin forming as soon as you start learning about money.

- They can be raised and lowered depending on how you respond to them.

What's Your Story

Now that you're aware of your Money Ceiling, it's time to work with it and raise it to new heights.

Step 1: Acknowledge that you have a ceiling. Owning it gives you the power to change it.

Step 2: Describe your ceiling. What's it made of? Which pieces are strongest—stories, emotions, identity, judgments? What other components does your ceiling have?

Step 3: Write or create images of what your ceiling looks like. What is its height?

Step 4: Now that you know what your money ceiling is made of take these actions to dismantle it piece by piece:

Stories: Recognize that those early messages were never yours. Forgive yourself for holding them and release them.

Emotions: Feel your emotions and process them. Fear and anxiety lose power the moment you stop running from them. Release the emotions that no longer serve you and stand tall and confident.

Identity: See how you defined yourself around money and create a new image. Build a vision board of who you are becoming.

Judgements: Catch yourself the moment you start comparing yourself to someone else. Comparison is judgment, and judgment is a sign that you're stuck. This is where Micro Moments of Change matter. When you're in the middle of a situation and you pause before reacting the way you always do, you break the automatic response your body and mind have practiced for years. That pause interrupts the old wiring. Every time you stop, breathe, and choose something different, you're actively updating your brain. These micro moments may feel small, but they are powerful. They are the real-time rewrites that shift your relationship with money from the inside out.

Language: Listen to the words you use when you talk or think about money. Your language is one of the clearest indicators of where your ceiling sits. And just like with judgment, this is where a Micro Moment of Change can shift everything. When you catch yourself using limiting or familiar phrases, pause. That single pause breaks the old pattern and gives you space to choose words that reflect where you're going, not where you've been. Every time you do this, you strengthen a new relationship with your financial well-being.

Self-Worth: Recognize and accept that you are a worthy, capable and deserving being. Again, use the micro moments of change technique whenever you have a doubt.

Awareness comes first. Practice carries you into the next version of yourself. Stay patient. Notice the changes as they arrive. They're evidence that your story is changing for good.

Chapter 9
Rewriting the Scripts – New Perspectives

"You can't live your life for other people. You've got to do what's right for you." —**Noah Calhoun – *The Notebook***

December 2023

I've always liked this time of year. I love the holidays, and I find this is a great time to pause and consider what's working. What's not and where I want to go next.

When I was writing Life Rewritten I was deep in my own story. I was digging through old patterns, memories and choices, examining them to see what if any still fit. That book was a big picture view of how we build our lives from the stories we tell ourselves. But as I worked on it, I started to notice something else. Each area of life comes with its own set of stories. Health, love, money, age, parenting all come with their own set of messages and expectations that we quietly absorb without even realizing it.

Money stood out the most for me. If I was going to put my work out in the world with confidence, I had to take a hard look at my own money stories. Where was I still getting stuck? Where was I keeping myself small or afraid? Once I started asking those questions, the answers came flooding in. Some of them hit hard.

When I got honest about my relationship with money, I realized I was standing at a crossroads. My life wasn't dreadful. I had good things happening. Sure I had my challenges and often woke up with my jaw aching from grinding my teeth. Wasn't that part of being a responsible adult? I'd always been someone who overthought things and held onto old hurts and future worries forever. Wasn't that a part of my wiring? Didn't that make me a regular human being? Besides I had so many gifts, so much to be grateful for. How could I possibly want more?

And then I admitted it. I did want more.

The second I said that truth out loud, the old voices went into overdrive.

"You're so GREEDY!"

"Be happy with what you have!"

"You always do this, stirring up the pot, and where does it get you? Broke and disappointed!"

Those words had lived in me for years. Most of my life really. But at that moment I didn't back down. Something in me was done.

That was the moment I decided to change, to stop listening to the noise, stop apologizing for wanting more and finally start owning what I really wanted. I chose to move forward. And I haven't looked back since.

A New Money Story

The thoughts I shared in the above story are the same ones I talk about in my courses on rewriting money scripts for women (Money Rewritten™ for Women). Those patterns kept me small. They held me back from bringing my real talents and gifts forward. Once I started doing the work I now bring to audiences, my life began to change. And it continues.

Some of the changes were hard. I had to let go of friendships that were rooted in staying small, in keeping things "comfortable." It was painful. But I've also gained deeper friendships and support who remind me that life is about showing up, fully participating, being present and being seen. My world has opened up in ways I used to only dreamed about. It's given me a voice I now use to help others.

It took practice and it took patience., two things I've never been great at. When I decided to move forward, I wanted immediate results. I wanted the universe to respond on my timeline. I would think, *I did the work, where are my ten new clients?*

But that's not how it works. In fact the opposite happened. As I worked on my money script, more challenges appeared than I ever imagined. Someone stole my identity and started writing checks in my name. The bank froze my account while they investigated. It wasn't just the money that was taken; it was my sense of safety and security that I needed to address.

The point is, everything that came up, every thought, challenge, or crisis, showed me exactly where I was on my path to a stronger financial future. It was my money script, playing out in real time. When I stepped back and observed instead of reacting, I shifted my awareness and, more importantly, my perspective.

When you change how you see the situation, it becomes feedback instead of judgment – insight instead of a stick to beat yourself with. That's the power of perspective. It helps you see meaning where you once saw mistakes and possibility where you once saw failure.

Because when something derails your plans, you fall into a state of emotional turmoil. You can't act. You can't change your behavior or mindset when you're agitated. When you're anxious and reactive, your brain moves into fight-or-flight mode, unable to focus on creativity or growth. Understanding this "lizard brain" response is fundamental to create lasting change.

The Plot Thickens

When you realize you're rewriting a script you've carried for most of your life, following these steps will bring the life you want closer—faster and with less stress. The purpose of the previous chapters has been to uncover where you are with your relationship with money. Now, armed with that awareness, you can begin to change who you are in relation to money, solidifying your bond and building a strong rapport.

Forgiveness: Forgiveness is one of the greatest gifts you can give yourself. Forgiveness sets you free. Forgiveness is not about forgetting or reconciliation. It's about understanding why you were choosing to let it go. If you're replaying conversations or events that still trigger you, forgiveness is the first step in quieting that noise.

The same applies to self-forgiveness. Most of you would never be friends with someone who judges and criticizes you the way you chide yourself. Practicing self-forgiveness means acknowledging the mistake, feeling the remorse, and accepting your humanity. It's the benchmark of accountability and character.

Applying forgiveness to your money story allows for greater awareness and the space for micro-moments of change. These seemingly small adjustments rewire your brain, reduce the power of triggers, and dissolve shame loops that keep you stuck. You need forgiveness to let go of the past and with it, the stories that held you back.

Gratitude: Gratitude is another powerful tool in your emotional tool kit. Gratitude literally changes your physiological and emotional state, calming the body and clearing the mind. I've given clients gratitude practices that produced swift breakthroughs, transforming difficult situations into successful outcomes.

Gratitude is a miracle in action. Take a moment now and feel grateful for something in your life. It could be as small as the chance to read these words or as grand as your new car or home. Notice what happened in your body and mind when you do. That's the power of gratitude.

Grief: Grief encompasses more than the loss of a loved one. Grief occurs any time your life changes shape. I remember when my sister moved out of her beloved home. She'd made the space a sanctuary; the decision to move was difficult. Ultimately, she wanted to start a new chapter; the sale of the home would support this. During those months, I watched her move through denial, anger, bargaining and finally acceptance.

To help her through this process, I suggested she record a video walkthrough of the home, thanking each room, her cherished garden and the memories she'd made. She created a lovely video with music, into one keepsake that she treasures to this day.

Understand that you, too, may feel grief when changing your relationship with money. Recognize it as a sign of the time and energy you've invested in an old identity. Feel it. Honor it. And then let it go so that you can welcome what's next.

Image/Identity: The way you imagine yourself is how you show up in the world. Your identity is not dissimilar as they both are comprised of the qualities and characteristics that make you a unique individual. While it includes your physical image, it's more significantly a mixture of the beliefs, attitudes and values that you hold and that are important to you.

When it comes to money, many of you in the service fields feel great pride in your work, but uncomfortable about the compensation. That's because the collective image says that being of service is more noble than being wealthy. Thinking about wanting more money can trigger guilt, shame, or fear of judgement.

Some religions claim that wealth is immoral – which is ironic considering how many religious institutions hold strong financial portfolios. If you follow a particular faith, be aware of how those teachings might influence your self-image around abundance.

You can change that story. Practice stepping into a new identity, one that's comfortable in wealth and worthiness.

Willingness to Receive: Receiving sounds simple enough — you do it every day. You receive packages from Amazon, texts from friends, emails that land in your inbox. But I want you to pause for a moment and come with me on this thought: *What if receiving is much deeper than simply taking in what shows up?*

Life was never meant to be as hard or painful as it's become for so many. Turn on the news, and it's overflowing with chaos and uncertainty. Yet what if life itself was always intended to be a gift — one designed to help you learn about yourself, make new choices, and redirect when the old ones stop serving you? What if it was meant to be rich with joy, ease, and abundance?

You live on a planet overflowing with gifts — beauty, resources, opportunities, connections. Yes, some have been damaged, polluted, or neglected. But even amid those realities, one essential truth often gets forgotten:

Life is a gift; yours is to receive it.

That may sound esoteric, and maybe it is, but look around — the world is built for abundance. The real question is:

Do you believe you deserve it?

Do you believe that simply by existing, you are worthy of the good that wants to find you?

That's where *willingness to receive* comes in. It's not just a mindset — it's a measure of how deeply you allow yourself to be supported by life. It reflects your beliefs about worthiness, deservability, and what you think you're "allowed" to have.

Can you open your hands and heart to the gifts already surrounding you — including money?

I don't believe anyone was meant to struggle endlessly. Yet struggle persists, often because we unconsciously resist receiving. This step is an invitation:

Consider how much of life's abundance you're willing to receive… and then allow yourself to receive even more.

Each of these steps requires repetition. Practicing them will not only change your reliance on the old rote responses, but it will also rewire your brain. Remember, you're building a new relationship with money it could take some time to break old habits and start new ones. Be patient and kind with yourself.

Plot Points

To recap:

- It is possible to change your relationship with money.

- You begin by knowing your current relationship with money.

- Once known, then you can create a new sense of self through forgiveness, gratitude, releasing grief, building a new image and receiving.

- Shifting your perspective shifts your story.

What's Your Story

Follow these steps to create a new version of yourself, one who enjoys a healthy, empowered relationship with money.

Step 1: For each elements above ask yourself the following questions. Be honest. Don't judge. Judgement keeps you stuck.

>*Forgiveness* – Who can I forgive right now for what they did or what I did? What happened? Why did it happen? Forgive.

>*Gratitude* – What are three things I am grateful for today?

>*Grief* – What am I holding onto because I haven't grieved it?

>*Image/Identity* – Do I see myself as a prosperous person? Take a moment and imagine yourself with financial peace and ask: How do I feel living a stress-free life?

>*Willing to Receive* – How much more of life's bounty am I willing to receive?

Step 2: After answering, notice what comes up. Did anything surprise you? One client discovered deep anger she'd been holding for years. She processed the anger and forgave. She then found freedom and within six months, launched a thriving a new business.

Step 3: After a week to ten days, repeat the process. Have your answers changed? Do you feel more connected, confident or engaged?

Step 4: Keep a journal or an image board tracking your success.

You've come a long way. You've named your stories, uncovered their origins, and rewritten the beliefs that kept you small. You've seen how money shows up in your life and you've started to shift how you respond to it.

Now comes the moment that matters most: what you do with all of this. Awareness is powerful, but action is where the real change happens. This is where your rewritten story moves from the page to your life — how you spend, save, speak, and show up in the world.

That's what comes next.

Chapter 10
And now?
Lasting Change

"It's what you do right now that makes a difference."
—Jeff Sanderson – *Black Hawk Down*

January 2025

It was finally coming together. My book, Life Rewritten, was done and would be launched in March. The remodel of our home, while disruptive, was well underway. I was making great money – enough to cover expenses, fund my book and business and plan for my next chapter. I was preparing to launch The Rewritten Collection, my new venture that would combine my story-based personal growth tools with my creative expressive side.

I was on podcasts almost twice a week and had several speaking engagements lined up. I barely recognized myself, so much had changed. My life was working.

Then one Friday afternoon, I felt a strange sensation come over me. It wasn't panic, and it wasn't the wild "make it happen!" drive I'd lived with for years. This was unfamiliar. It was quiet. Still. It took me a moment to realize what it was.

I was happy.

It wasn't a manic high, and it wasn't tied to me achieving something. It was a grounded peaceful happiness. It felt balanced. Like ease. Like finally being able to breathe without waiting for the next shoe to drop.

Simon and I were in a great place. Our dog, Samworf, filled our lives with a tremendous amount of joy. I'd never felt that kind of calm, so I paused. I let it in. I let it sit in my chest. I wanted to memorize it, to anchor it. Because, for the first time, I could see what I had created: a life that reflected who I truly was.

I knew that I would still face challenges. Life isn't about perfection; it's about how you respond when crisis shows up. And that was the shift. In the past, I'd spiral, overthink or fight against reality. Now, I could breathe, assess and choose a different way. The great revelation was that I didn't have to be perfect. I just had to do enough, keep showing up, and stay present and my life would change.

The more I practiced, the more my life opened up. I could see the evidence everywhere — new clients, creative collaborations, new levels of trust in myself. It was working. My life was working. It was time to bring what I learned out into the world and help others do the same.

And so I did.

From Awareness to Action

Everything you've read so far has been designed to help you transform your relationship with money, not in theory, but in practice. From your Money Ceiling, the language you use when you talk or think about money, and the hidden beliefs that determine how you receive and manage it.

Now it's time to take inspired action to apply what you've discovered. Because insight without action just becomes another form of avoidance.

When I teach my *Money Rewritten*™ programs this is where the real transformation begins. People walk away with powerful realizations: "I see how my mother's fear became my fear" or "I finally understand why I push money away." But when they start practicing new language, new behaviors, and new ways of responding, their lives start to change in significant ways.

Take "Marta," for example. After one of my courses, she decided to start working with her money instead of avoiding it. For the first time in her life, she sat down and created a budget – nothing fancy, just a clear look at what was coming in and what was going out. And for the first time in her life, she felt calm about it.

In the past, the thought of logging into her bank account made her stomach churn. She'd grab a coffee, scroll her social media accounts or call a friend – anything to avoid facing her finances. But this time, she stayed. She took a deep breath and looked at the numbers as information – not a way to judge herself.

Inspired, Marta met with a financial planner, ready to take the next logical step. The financial planner criticized her budget, told her that she was "too far behind," and that at forty-five, she didn't have enough time to reach her goals. Marta was crushed. She was certain she'd failed again, convinced nothing would work for her. Luckily, Marta remembered my advice on micro-moments of change. She took a deep breath and decided to call me and asked for help rather than go down this once familiar path.

When she finished telling me what happened, I said, "Congratulations!"

At first she laughed, thinking I was joking. Then said, "You're serious aren't you?"

I was. Because at that very moment, the sting of disappointment fresh in her mind and body, was actually proof that she was changing.

When you begin rewriting your money story, life responds. It gives you insights into where to go even deeper and heal even more. This financial planner wasn't her enemy. He was her mirror voicing every doubt and criticism she silently believed about herself for years. Now that she heard them out loud, she could see them for what they were – old stories. Not truth.

It changed everything. For Marta it was about her identity. Did she really see herself as a someone that handled money well. In this case, the answer was no.

She began to view her finances not as punishment, but as a partnership. She stopped using avoidance to cope and started embracing awareness. Within six months, she'd grown her savings, paid of an old credit card and landed two new freelance clients that doubled her income.

This is how the work functions. You change the inside first, then the outside follows.

The truth is, life gives us constant feedback about where we are in our story. Every bill, every windfall, every delay, every "no" or "not yet" — they're all forms of communication. When you stop taking them as punishment and start viewing them as data, you step into power.

Think of it like a report card, not a reprimand. Feedback tells you where to focus your attention. It helps you identify which patterns still need your care.

If you can ask yourself, *What if this is here to help me?* instead of *What's wrong with me?,* everything changes. The moment you do that, you shift from judgment to discernment — from being the victim of your story to being its author again.

Roles That Shape Money Scripts

As you keep doing this work, something starts to show itself that you may not have noticed before. Your relationship with money isn't one thing. It changes depending on the role you're in. The version of you who runs a business can feel strong and clear about money, and the version of you at home can feel guilty or hesitant about spending on yourself. Your scripts live in your identities, how you see yourself. Every identity comes with its own set of expectations and emotions.

Women feel this in a very unique way: don't be too much. Don't make too much. Don't want too much. Be grateful. Be helpful. Don't outshine anyone. It's subtle, but it's there, and it shows up in who gets to make the financial decisions and who's expected to adapt. That conflict between ambition and obligation is real. You want more but you also don't want to break the rules you were given. That's why I created Money Rewritten for Women — because those rules were never meant to guide grown, capable women building their own lives.

Entrepreneurs live inside a totally different emotional story. There's ambition. You're building something, so of course you want it to grow. But right next to ambition is survival. Anyone in this role knows how quickly your confidence can disappear when the numbers drop. Some months you feel unstoppable. Other months you stare at your bank balance and feel the old panic in your stomach. Envy shows up when you compare yourself to others that seem to succeed so easily. And entitlement — the healthy version that says that everyone deserves — often gets buried under self-doubt. This is how entrepreneurs end up building their businesses from fear instead of trust.

Executives and leaders have their own version of this inner conflict. On the outside you're strong, grounded, successful, the one everyone depends on. But living that role comes with its own emotional baggage. Obligation weighs on you. Fairness shows up as "I shouldn't complain; look how lucky I am." Ambition pushes you forward, but safety pulls you back. You're expected to take risks and also protect everyone else around you. It's a tug-of-war that most leaders feel but rarely discuss.

Artists/Creative have another old story entirely. This one says that struggle is part of the deal. That starving-artist myth haunts you. It tells you that if you're not suffering for your art, it doesn't count. That prosperity ruins your authentic soul. It's ridiculous, but it's powerful. So ambition gets dampened, survival becomes the norm, and any desire for more feels like betrayal. Creativity is abundance in motion. But if your script says abundance corrupts, you hold yourself back without even noticing.

Then there are the healers, coaches, teachers, and support professionals. Obligation is their primary focus. Fairness, too. You're supposed to give. You're supposed to show up. There's nothing wrong with that, but so many people in these roles confuse compassion with sacrifice. They undercharge, over deliver, and call it generosity. Risk feels selfish, safety feels noble. And when someone in the same field charges well and grows, envy and guilt take over. It's a tightrope act. But the truth is simple: you serve better when you're valued. The value starts with you.

Here's the thing that ties all of this together: you're not just one of these roles; you are several of them all the time.

You might be a business owner and a parent. A coach and an artist; a parent and a spouse/partner. Every role has its own emotional story, rules, fears and definition of "enough." They can pull you in opposite directions:

- Ambition versus obligation.
- Risk versus safety.
- Fairness versus negative entitlement.
- Envy versus gratitude.
- Survival versus expansion.

Each of these roles can either expand or restrict your financial flow. When you identify the scripts tied to each role, you can choose which ones stay and which ones go. That's how you begin to improve your relationship with money — consciously, intentionally, and with grace.

The Plot Thickens

You've done the deep work — uncovered the emotions, beliefs, and behaviors that have shaped your financial life. You've confronted the parts of your story that once scared you. You've found language that honors your truth.

Now it's time to turn awareness into structure. Because clarity without movement changes nothing.

1. **Build a New Financial Strategy:** Create a fresh relationship with your money. Look at your financial planning, not as a cage, but as a roadmap. It doesn't limit you — it directs you. Notice how you feel when you make financial decisions. Your emotions are information.

2. **Take Inspired Action:** When something feels aligned, move toward it. You don't need every answer before you begin. Confidence doesn't come from certainty — it comes from motion.

3. **Make a Plan for Growth:** Wealth is built on intention. Map out your goals — saving, investing, earning — and align them with your values. A plan rooted in self-worth grows faster than one rooted in fear

4. **Hire a Trusted Advisor:** You don't have to do this alone. Surround yourself with professionals who respect your goals, your boundaries, and your values. The right advisor should empower you, not intimidate you.

5. **Educate Yourself:** Learn the basics of how money moves — what interest really means, how investments grow, how to read your statements. Knowledge builds confidence, and confidence builds stability.

6. **Create New Habits That Stick:** Set systems that reflect your new beliefs. Automate your savings. Track your progress monthly. Celebrate small wins. These habits tell your subconscious; this is who I am now.

7. **Keep Walking Toward Abundance:** You're not chasing perfection; you're building consistency. Each conscious choice — no matter how small — shifts your trajectory.

8. **Watch Your Savings Grow:** Let your results reflect your new story. Every dollar saved, every smart choice made, is proof that your inner work is translating into real-world abundance.

9. **Practice Gratitude:** Gratitude is your anchor. It keeps abundance grounded in joy rather than fear. Acknowledge every bit of progress — every bill paid, every unexpected blessing.

10. **Pay Attention:** As you bring more of these changes into your life, pay attention to the signs that show your progress. Even when something feels difficult, remember it's not a setback — it's insight. What you notice now is exactly what you're ready to address. Acknowledge it, trust yourself, and keep moving forward.

Synchronicity: The Quiet Proof

As you begin living from your new money story, pay attention to what starts showing up around you. Sometimes, the first signs that your relationship with money is changing are small — a refund you forgot about, a new client who feels like a perfect fit, a conversation that opens a door you didn't even know was there. That's synchronicity.

Synchronicity isn't luck; it's alignment. It's the universe's quiet way of showing you that your energy, actions, and beliefs are finally in sync. It's confirmation that you're no longer chasing, but allowing. When you notice these moments, pause and acknowledge them. They're your evidence that the work you've done is working.

The more you recognize these subtle shifts, the stronger your trust grows — in yourself, your choices, and your ability to create abundance with ease.

The Emotional Reality of Change

It's easy to romanticize growth — to make it sound smooth and linear. It's not. Sometimes it's messy. You'll have days when you slip back into old patterns. That doesn't mean you've failed. It means you're human.

What matters is that you catch it faster, recover sooner, and move forward with compassion.

Growth is emotional. When you change your money story, you're also changing your identity, your relationships, and your sense of safety. That's why patience and grace are essential. Every emotional wave is part of the healing.

When you hit resistance — when an old voice whispers "who do you think you are?" — that's not sabotage. That's your nervous system adjusting to your new story. Breathe through it. Acknowledge it. And keep going.

Plot Points

To recap:

- You've uncovered your old story and written a new one. Now it's time to live it.

- Every challenge is feedback — a signpost pointing toward your next level of awareness.

- Support matters. Coaches, friends, and mentors help you stay grounded as you grow.

- Each decision, each small act of courage, is proof that your story is rewriting itself in real time.

What's Your Money Story Today?

Pause here. Take a deep breath. Look at how far you've come — not just in what you've learned, but in how you see yourself.

You've faced your patterns. You've questioned the beliefs that shaped you. You've built a new relationship with money — one that feels grounded, honest, and aligned with who you are now.

This is your rewrite in motion.

As you continue to navigate this new you consider the following:

Step 1: What does abundance mean to me — right now, in this moment?

Step 2: How has my language around money changed since I began this journey?

Step 3: Which new habits already feel natural, and which still need attention?

Step 4: What financial action will I take this month that reflects my new story?

Step 5: What emotions do I want to feel each time I make, spend, or save money?

Step 6: Who am I becoming as I continue this rewrite?

Your money story doesn't end here. It evolves with every decision, every deposit, every moment of awareness. You have the tools, the insight, and the power. Keep rewriting. Keep expanding. Keep allowing abundance to meet you where you now stand — confident, capable, and fully aligned with your worth.

You've rewritten your story, but remember, the story keeps unfolding. There's one more practice that ties it all together and prepares you for what's ahead.

Bonus Step: Future Gratitude

Before you close this chapter, take one more step forward. Future Gratitude is exactly what it sounds like — gratitude for the life that's already unfolding ahead of you. Take a moment and imagine how it feels when the changes you've made in your relationship with money have taken root. You're living with financial freedom. You make choices based on desire and alignment rather than fear or obligation. You no longer feel trapped in the endless loop of budget, save, spend, repeat.

Pause and really feel that. What does it look like? What emotions come up when you picture yourself there — calm, confident, and capable? Let that version of you speak. Then, add gratitude. Thank yourself for doing the work that got you here. Thank the opportunities that have yet to arrive.

Your future already exists; it's waiting for you to meet it. When you practice gratitude for the future you're calling in, you bridge the space between where you are and where you're going. Gratitude anchors possibility into reality — and that's how you start living the next chapter of your story today.

Bonus Chapter: The 90 Day Money Rewrite Challenge

You do not need more motivation or willpower. You do not need a perfect budget and a new spreadsheet. If money feels burdensome in your life, it is rarely because you do not know what to do. It is because the story holding your money decisions has been running the show, and you have been trying to function in a story that holds you back instead of giving you the support you need for success.

A 90-day challenge gives you something a 30-day reset cannot. Thirty days can create awareness and spark momentum, but a 90-day process changes old patterns. It gives you time to notice the script, try a new behavior, watch your somatic responses, and then practice again until the updated actions become your new familiar. That is where real change happens.

This challenge is built to be simple enough to follow, but deep enough to create change that lasts. It does not ask you to do everything at once. It asks you to build consistency in how you relate to money, because your relationship with money is what defines the outcomes.

You will move through three phases. Each phase lasts 30 days, which makes this easy to track and easy to commit to. You are not chasing perfection. You are building a new way of being with money that becomes your identity.

How to use the challenge

Pick a time of day that works. Ten minutes is enough, and more is welcome if you have it. Some days will be reflective, some will be practical, and some will be about regulation and identity. If you miss a day, do not start over. The old money story loves re-start energy because restart energy is an excuse to stop. Just pick up where you left off.

I've listed the days and also provided a chart on my website for each 30 days that you can use as a guide outside of the book.

Keep one notebook, recording or image board for this. Do not scatter it across your phone, sticky notes, and half-finished journals. Give your money story one place to live so you can see it clearly.

One more thing. You do not need to do every task perfectly. The point is to show up long enough for the truth to surface and real change to take seed and grow.

Phase 1: Days 1 to 30
Awareness and Truth Telling

The first month is about identifying what is running your money life. This is where you discover your money script. The goal is not to judge your habits. The goal is to recognize and acknowledge them.

Day 1   Write your current money story as you see it. Don't hold back or try to sugarcoat it.

Day 2   What do you believe about money and people who have it.

Day 3   Set a money intention for the month. Example: I want to feel calm when I look at my bank account.

Day 4   Identify where your beliefs came from. Parents, culture, religion, class, partners, past experiences.

Day 5   Choose one limiting belief and write a new version. Consider: what would having enough feel like, and what would it change.

Day 6   Practice the affirmation: I am safe, supported, and open to receiving.

Day 7   Gratitude: list five things money has made possible in your life.

Day 8   Visualize your future self. How do you interact with money, and what feels different.

Day 9   Track all spending today with no judgment. This is data.

Day 10   Write a letter to money as if it were a person.

Day 11   Do three minutes of breathwork or grounding before any money related decision.

Day 12   Replace one sentence you use often such as *"I can't afford that"* with *"that is not a priority for me right now."*

Day 13   Review your bank account and say thank you for every cent.

Day 14   Affirmation: I am rewriting what success and security look like for me.

Day 15   Celebrate a small financial win, even if it is one choice you made with intention.

Day 16   Spend five dollars or less on something that brings you joy, and do not justify it.

Day 17   Declutter your wallet or your money space. Create calm where your money lives.

Day 18   Write three things about yourself that are valuable and cannot be bought.

Day 19   Choose a mantra for the week. Example: money flows to me with ease and purpose.

Day 20   Make one money decision that feels aligned, not pressured.

Day 21   Check in. How do you feel about your money story now compared to Day 1.

Day 22 Create a simple vision board that represents financial ease.

Day 23 Share what you have learned with someone you trust, or journal it as if you are telling a friend.

Day 24 Pick one recurring expense to reassess or cancel with love.

Day 25 Take a money walk. Walk and think about how money supports your values.

Day 26 Write: I release shame and fear around money. I choose trust.

Day 27 Write a future journal entry from one year from now as if your relationship with money is steady.

Day 28 Reflect: what would financial peace look like day to day.

Day 29 Choose a story you are still holding that does not serve you, and write a new one.

Day 30 Celebrate your progress and acknowledge what has changed when you think about money.

At the end of Phase 1, you should have clarity on your patterns. You should also have proof that your money life is not something that happens to you. It follows a script. Now you will work on the part most people avoid.

Phase 2: Days 31 to 60
From Reaction to Choice

During these thirty days, you will take the awareness you found and start building a different response. Your money story is not only mental, but also physical. It is the tightening in your chest and throat before you open an email. It is the clenching in your jaw when you check your account. It is the urge to avoid, spend, freeze, or justify.

During these thirty days, you will practice staying present with money. It's where you'll start rewiring your brain's responses by practicing micro moments of change.

Day 31   Identify your money stress signals. Where do you feel it in your body.

Day 32   Create a one-minute micro moment of change: breath, shoulders down, feet on the floor, slow exhale. Practice this at times of stress.

Day 33   Choose one money moment you avoid and face it in the smallest way. Open the account. Look at one number. Don't linger.

Day 34   Name your default money response: avoid, control, overwork, overspend, please others, freeze/do nothing.

Day 35   Practice a pause before spending today. No change required, just pause.

Day 36   Write/record/image: what do I fear will happen if I slow down with money.

Day 37 Create a money boundary for the week. One simple one will suffice

Day 38 Do a clean review of subscriptions and auto payments. Keep what matches your values and close the rest.

Day 39 Ask: what do I do with money when I feel emotional. Recognize the pattern.

Day 40 Choose one soothing practice and pair it with a money practice. For example, sit in nature and check out your bank balance on your app.

Day 41 Write a new response line for your biggest money trigger. Example: Thank you for showing me what I used to do. I now relax and make a new choice.

Day 42 Practice receiving. Accept a compliment, help, or support with a simple thank you.

Day 43 Decide on one small amount to save weekly. Keep it easy enough to succeed.

Day 44 Plan for the extra money that is now showing up. Create a savings account for a special treat or to pay down debt. This gives your new relationship purpose.

Day 45 Review the wins that have already happened. Note what you did differently without dismissing it.

Day 46 Identify a money loyalty. Who do you fear outgrowing or losing as your money story changes.

Day 47 Rewrite that loyalty into a new way of being. Example: I can belong and still have more.

Day 48 Practice a calm money check in. Look at your account and take three slow breaths.

Day 49 Choose one spending habit that is not aligned and adjust. For example, check how many subscriptions you have and keep only what you use and need.

Day 50 Do one money task you have delayed and complete it. For example, many people delay income tax filing simply because they aren't ready to "deal" with taxes.

Day 51 Notice how you talk about money. Clean up one overused phrase.

Day 52 Write/record/image: what would a steady relationship with money look like for me.

Day 53 Practice asking. Ask for what you need in one area of your life.

Day 54 Set a simple plan for a bill, debt, or savings goal. Keep it realistic.

Day 55 Celebrate calm. Calm is a win.

Day 56 Identify where you feel money defines your worth. Write the belief that attaches money to worth.

Day 57 Choose a replacement belief that fits for you.

Day 58 Practice discomfort. Do one money task while staying present.

Day 59 Evaluate your month. What triggers have lessened. What still causes distress.

Day 60 Commit to the identity you are building. Name it in one sentence.

By the end of Phase 2, your goal is not that you never feel fear. Your goal is that fear stops driving your choices. You can feel the emotion and still choose a response that supports you.

Now the final month solidifies your new relationship with money.

Phase 3: Days 61 to 90
Identity and Wealth Practice

This month is where you move from change as a concept to a new way of being. Many people can do a reset. Fewer can make it a new identity. This is where you build the person who can keep it.

You will practice being someone who holds money with steadiness, makes decisions without panic, and receives with ease.

Day 61   Define wealth for you. How do you now see yourself in relationship to money.

Day 62   Write the traits of your wealth identity. How you act, how do you make choices.

Day 63   Choose one new trait and practice it today.

Day 64   Review your pricing, earning, or income story. What is your ceiling.

Day 65   Write a new ceiling statement that feels possible.

Day 66   Identify your money behaviors. What is no longer acceptable.

Day 67   Create one new behavior and practice it once.

Day 68   Choose one way to increase your receiving. Raise a rate, accept help, accept a compliment, accept a yes.

Day 69   Map your next ninety days after this challenge. What support do you need.

Day 70 Do a mid-month review and adjust.

Day 71 Write your old identity line around money. Then write the new one underneath it.

Day 72 Create a simple wealth routine that takes ten minutes a week.

Day 73 Choose one savings or investment action that supports future you.

Day 74 Do one act of leadership with money. Make the call, send the email, handle what you've been avoiding.

Day 75 Celebrate being the person who follows through.

Day 76 Identify where you still perform to earn money. Decide what you will stop doing.

Day 77 Practice clean receiving again. No explanation, no stress.

Day 78 Make one money decision from values, not fear.

Day 79 Write/record/image: what would I do if I trusted money could support me.

Day 80 Take one action from that list.

Day 81 Review the full ninety days. Name the biggest shift.

Day 82 Write your new money story in one page.

Day 83 Identify the practices you will keep for the next month.

Day 84 Identify the habits you are done with and why.

Day 85 Create a plan for the next time you slip. No shame, just a plan.

Day 86 Write a letter from your future self to your current self.

Day 87 Choose a celebration that matches your values, not a spending splurge.

Day 88 Share your shift with someone you trust, or write it as if you are teaching it.

Day 89 Decide what support would help you keep going: community, coaching, accountability, structure.

Day 90 Close the challenge by naming who you are now in relation to money.

Closing

A 90-day challenge is not about doing everything right. It is about staying with the new perspective and then choosing a new response often enough that it becomes natural. If money has been heavy in your life, this gives you a clean way to put the weight down, not through denial, but through practice.

You do not need to become a different person to have a different money life. You need to stop living inside a story that makes money a threat, a judge, or a constant problem to solve. When that storyline loosens, money becomes what it has always been.

A resource that can support the life you desire.

If you want to use this as a group program, you can turn it into weekly check-ins with one theme per week, plus daily prompts. If you want to use it privately, follow the days in order and keep the focus on consistency.

Ninety days is enough time to see yourself clearly, interrupt the old patterns, and begin living from a new one.

Congratulations! You made it.

Epilogue

As I worked on this epilogue, I kept thinking about where I was when I began, how much of my own money story was still up in the air. Even after all the work I've done, I'm still rewriting it. I still notice old fears. I still hear the old beliefs I carried for decades. But what's different now is how quickly I recognize the story. What used to take me down for days barely registers now. That's the gift of awareness. It doesn't erase your past, but it puts you back in charge.

And here's what I want you to know as you close this book: once your money story begins to change, everything else begins to change with it.

At first, it's subtle. Your body doesn't clench the way it used to. You breathe a little deeper. Your health improves because you're not carrying a lifetime of financial stress in your nervous system. There's more ease, more peace, more room to just be.

Then you notice it in your relationships. You communicate differently because you're no longer speaking from fear or guilt. Your words lose the charge that others feel without knowing why. You stop apologizing for your needs. You stop shrinking to make others comfortable. You choose different partners, friends, boundaries. You find yourself less reactive, more grounded, more honest.

Work shifts too. Careers that once dragged you down now lift you. Decisions become clearer. You take opportunities you would have talked yourself out of before. You set boundaries you once feared setting. One day you notice that the world responds to you in a new way and realize it's because you are different, you've changed.

As much as this work transforms your inner world, it doesn't end there. Your rewrite influences the people around you. Your children watch you make decisions from confidence, not scarcity. Your partner feels that you're grounded and at peace. Friends notice how your language and your voice shift. The people closest to you begin to rethink their own stories simply because you rewrote yours.

This is how generational narratives change. One person becomes aware. One person stops repeating what was handed down. One person says, "This ends with me." And that is enough to open a door for everyone who comes after.

Yes, this work is personal. It asks you to look at parts of yourself you may have avoided for years. But once you do, the transformation is unmistakable. You don't just change your relationship with money — you change your relationship with yourself, your world, and the possibilities you once believed were out of reach.

You've done the work. You've seen your story. You've created space for something new. Now you get to live this new version and let it move outward into every chapter of your life.

This isn't the end. It's the new beginning.

You are the author of your money story. Own it.

And when you look back on this a year from now, imagine the story you'll be telling then.

Acknowledgements

As a writer, I always thought the hardest part of finishing a book was staring at the blank page. I was wrong. The real work begins after you hit save.

Bringing a book into the world takes far more than one manuscript. It takes belief, patience, perspective, and people willing to stand with you when the work feels uncertain or unfinished. I have been incredibly fortunate to be surrounded by just such people.

Simon Knight, my partner in all parts of life.

Thelma Alane, my sister and lifelong friend.

Zoë Landers, my dear friend and fellow magician.

I am deeply grateful to my friends John Lavack and Roberto Blain for their unwavering support and for always being willing to take my calls when doubt and fear clouded my thinking.

Brian Werdesheim, Robert Dalie, and the late Jim Miles opened my eyes more than twenty years ago to a different way of understanding money and its role in our lives. Their influence shaped this work in ways that run far deeper than these pages. Brian's foreword to this book truly was icing on the cake.

I would not have crossed the finish line without Linda Fisk, Amanda Taylor, and Lisa Apolinski. Your belief in this work, especially when it mattered most, always came at the most needed times.

There were countless other individuals who helped me on this journey: Michal McCracken, Diana Benzaquen, Michael Beas, Schiammarelly Pinckert Nieme, Fabiana Barbery, Chris Colt, Janice Edwards, John Lavack and Phillip Ludlow to name but a few.

To the financial professionals and thinkers who share my belief that anyone can change the role money plays in their life. I could not agree more, and this book exists because of that shared knowing.

Finally, to you, the reader. Thank you for choosing this book and for putting your trust in me. I hope you found clarity, possibility, and a new way of relating to money that truly serves you.

About the Author

Carrie KC West has spent her life immersed in the transformative power of stories. Her journey began long before earning a Master of Fine Arts in filmmaking from the prestigious American Film Institute, where she spent two intensive years honing the craft of storytelling. As a script and book reader for production companies, she dissected the structure, themes, and characters of countless stories, uncovering what made them resonate or fall flat.

Carrie's analytical skills extend far beyond the world of film. Before and after her time at AFI, she worked with organizations to evaluate and optimize business processes. It was during this work that she discovered how businesses operate much like stories, guided by characters, arcs, and themes that drive their successes or failures. This insight inspired her upcoming book, *Business Rewritten.*

Carrie's academic background also includes a Bachelor of Science in counseling psychology from Penn State University, which deepened her understanding of human behavior. This foundation sharpened her ability to read people, a skill she first developed as a survival mechanism during a challenging childhood. Those experiences taught her how to navigate relationships, find belonging, and ultimately use those lessons to help others.

Carrie's commitment to personal growth is rooted in firsthand experience. She has explored therapy in its many forms, group, individual, psychoanalysis, and has delved into personal growth workshops and metaphysical practices. Her studies in Integrated Body Psychotherapy (IBP), tapping, and hypnotherapy revealed one powerful truth: storytelling is the key to understanding and changing our lives, even when it is not explicitly named.

Driven by the marvel of human resilience, Carrie believes that if she could turn the pain and challenges of her early years into the life she leads today, then change is possible for anyone. Her first book, the award-winning Life Rewritten, was born from her experience, study, and passion for storytelling as a tool for profound change.

Out of that came *The Rewritten Collection* which focuses on the hidden narratives that influence what we do, what we avoid and what we repeat. Money Rewritten is the latest book in this series. In Life Rewritten, she gives readers a practical way to recognize inherited and learned stories and replace them with choices that match who they are now. In Money Rewritten, she brings that same lens to finances, showing how money patterns are built from identity, emotion, and lived experience, not willpower alone. With clear tools and direct exercises, she helps readers name the script beneath their habits, trace where it began, and build a new relationship with money that holds up in real life.

Carrie KC West is the author of *Life Rewritten* and *Money Rewritten,* and the creator of *The Rewritten Collection.* Her work helps people change the script behind their decisions so money, health, relationships, and work start moving.

For additional help, PDF downloads, resources and information on scheduling a private session, visit my website, carriekcwest.com, where you will find more ideas and support. For your convenience, please use the QR Code below:

www.ingramcontent.com/pod-product-compliance
Lightning Source LLC
Chambersburg PA
CBHW052351030726
47602CB00016B/177/J